Also by Bryony Gordon:
The Wrong Knickers: A Decade of Chaos
Mad Girl: A Happy Life With a Mixed-Up Mind

EAT, DRINK,
RUN.

BRYONY GORDON

EAT, DRiNK, RUN.

HEADLINE

First published in 2018
by HEADLINE PUBLISHING GROUP

1

Cataloguing in Publication Data is available from the British Library

Hardback ISBN 978 1 4722 3402 5

Typeset in Berling by Palimpsest Book Production Ltd, Falkirk, Stirlingshire

Printed and bound in Great Britain by Clays Ltd, St Ives plc

Headline's policy is to use papers that are natural, renewable and recyclable
products and made from wood grown in sustainable forests. The logging and
manufacturing processes are expected to conform to the environmental
regulations of the country of origin.

HEADLINE PUBLISHING GROUP
An Hachette UK Company
Carmelite House
50 Victoria Embankment
London
EC4Y 0DZ

www.headline.co.uk
www.hachette.co.uk

For Harry

Contents

Prologue

I never thought I was a runner.

I was (am) a dawdler, a loafer, a drinker, a smoker. A dreamer, a screamer, and occasionally, when the mood takes me and I have had a few beers, a Belieber. A watcher of box sets, an eater of Scotch eggs. A cook in the living room (I love a TV dinner), a whore in the kitchen (you should see my hobs) and a maid in the bedroom (and by maid I mean . . . well no, you don't need to know about my sexual proclivities *just* yet. We have, after all, only just met).

I had done some running in my life, of course. I had run for a bus. I had run after unsuitable people: drug dealers, married men, blokes whose idea of kindness was to reply to a post-coital text only once I had sent 600 of my own checking they were still alive (for a long time during my twenties, I was so desperately sad that I often preferred to imagine the objects of my affection dead in a terrible accident than face the fact they just weren't that into me). Once I gave flight after a courier who had shoved a card through my door despite the fact I was in the flat at the time and had also gone to the trouble of specifying a safe place for him to leave my package (behind the bins, though I only chose this after I had been informed that, while my therapist's office may indeed be *my* safe place, it wasn't very practical as somewhere to deposit important bits of post given that it was in a hospital four miles away). I have spent a lot of time chasing daydreams, rainbows, and, in the words of the mighty Adele, pavements (usually several sheets to the wind. The bruises!). I would run for miles, or maybe more realistically a few metres, for a free doughnut. The years 2013 to present have mostly been spent running after a small child who for a worrying period thought it hysterically funny to sprint towards the road, me huffing and puffing wildly behind her, just about managing to scream her name, wondering how the fuck I managed to give birth to the baby equivalent of Usain Bolt, and whether one of those runners on the common wouldn't mind halting their judgemental thoughts about my inability to parent for just a minute and instead STOP MY CHILD FROM DASHING INTO THE PATH OF THAT ARTICULATED LORRY

THANK YOU VERY MUCH. (This has often led me to wonder when, exactly, the desire to move manically leaves us. Is it when we discover Nintendo, or when we discover wanking? Why do we tell our children to sit still all the time? Shouldn't we be saying to them, in the immortal words of S Club: don't stop movin' to the funky funky beat! It might be too late for us, paralysed by the constant refrains from our parents to sit still, but it's not too late for you, my child! Run free! Run wild! Just not *too* wild and nowhere near roads if that would be at all possible!)

But I digress. You should know now that I am really good at digressing, if not running. I was, of course, always well aware that running existed as a concept, as a thing people did to apparently make themselves feel better, but I didn't trust those people. I wasn't entirely sure that I wanted to be their friend.

As a young journalist in my twenties I would see joggers whizzing around the streets in the early morning as I returned home from a night out, the self-loathing seeping into my bones as the sun rose alongside their sap. Later, as a new mum, I would push my daughter around parks, watching people gallop around me like horses. These were people who didn't have tits like soggy sandbags, people unburdened by slack pelvic floors. I thought these people were weird, truth be told. Imagine actually *wanting* to exercise, actually choosing to do that instead of, say, sleep or eat cake or watch *Gossip Girl*. It wasn't something that had ever occurred to me other than as a form of torture, a symptom of the bulimia I carried around with me for most of my twenties and some of my thirties. Rarely – very rarely – I would dream about running, though really this was a form of nostalgia, a way of harking back to the time when I was four stone lighter and had no idea how slim and fit I was. But, as a 105-kilo woman with a penchant for beer and fags, these were dreams of what-could-have-been, not what-might-be.

So yes. I was not a runner. Until, one day, I realised that I was.

But this is not a book about running, despite the previous 1,000 words suggesting otherwise. It is a book about lots of things – drinking, smoking, eating, living – for people who think they can't run, though you could just as well take the word 'run' and replace it with any verb that puts the fear of God up you: learning French; asking someone on a date; getting on a plane; speaking in public; stitching a quilt. It's a book for people who think they can't swim, play tennis, practise yoga or do a handstand. (True story: I did my first handstand at the age of thirty-six and three quarters, on three hours' sleep and seven pints of lager. I would not recommend it.) It's a book for anyone who has spent their life thinking that they can't do things, despite the fact that they absolutely emphatically *can* (as long as it's within scientific reason and legal, though even the latter point is up for debate as long as you're happy to spend some time as a guest of Her Majesty).

I'm not one of those people given to posting inspirational quotes on Instagram, because I can think of things you'd rather have clogging up your feed (even pictures of coffee are preferable to someone misattributing a Shakespeare quote to a contestant from *Love Island*). But seeing as we're here, let me ask you: who put the T in can't, eh? Was it the teacher who said you would never amount to anything, the bully who stole your lunch money, the man who broke your heart, the parent who never showed you love? Or was it . . . you? You can-can-can do the can can. The only real limitations have been placed there by you, even if they did happen to get placed there by way of a terrible upbringing or a shitty boyfriend.

If I had a pound for every time someone has said to me, 'I'm not a runner/swimmer/person who does exercise', then I would not be sitting here in this coffee shop drinking my umpteenth flat white of the day, writing this book. I would be in my villa in the Bahamas, ordering my man-servant to make me another martini, even though I don't really drink martinis because my only experience of them ended with me face down in a stranger's lap. I would be shopping on Sloane Street or sailing the seven seas on a superyacht that would make all other superyachts look like Sainsbury's bath toys. It saddens me how quickly we announce that we can't do things – even more so because usually these statements are made on the shakiest of evidence presented to us by the gremlins in our own heads, who, by the way, are not lawyers for the state but figments of our poor self-esteem. And then there are the frankly unhelpful representations in the media of what a runner looks like – usually thin but ripped, tall and rangy. This morning I went out for a little run because I was feeling a bit sad and I knew that if I went out for a little run it might not stop me feeling a bit sad but it would at least show my sadness that I was *trying* to stop it, which is sometimes just as useful. I passed a Nike advert that was all about finding 'LONDON'S FASTEST!' It featured people with washboard stomachs wearing minuscule Nike crop tops. 'Don't want to be first? THEN JOG ON!' was one of the slogans. I stood in front of it and do you know what I thought? I thought, 'Fuck you, Nike! Fuck you VERY MUCH. Fuck you from all the people who pass this every day who might have been thinking about going for their first jog, but now feel too intimidated to. Fuck you from all of us who walk faster than we run. Fuck you from all of us who deserve medals not because we are fucking fast, but because we are out here and we are doing it EVEN THOUGH WE ARE SLOW. Fuck you and your stupid crop tops and watch as I fail to give a shit how long it takes me to run a mile!'

When you say you're not a runner, what you really mean is: you don't think you fit the profile of a runner. You don't look like the people in the Nike adverts. You can't fill a crop top or, like me, you can fill at least four crop tops. Also, people often mistake not being able to run with not *wanting* to run. But nobody actually wants to run, unless they are quite, quite strange. Believe me when I tell you that initially, absolutely everybody feels as if they are about to die when they so much as break into a light trot. Even those people who regularly go out for jogs will tell you that they don't actually want to beforehand – the difference between those people and the rest of us is that they have realised they never regret going for one afterwards.

Truth is, anyone with two functioning legs can run. Stick a zombie apocalypse behind you, and you will run. Put you in a field of angry cows, and you will run. Place you within touching distance of Donald Trump's hands, and you will run. It doesn't matter how fast or slowly you do it – the only thing that really matters is that you are doing it at all.

This makes me sound wise, when in actual fact it has taken me a long time to realise all this. A very long time. The only real reason I had this epiphany was because of the last book I wrote, and the absolutely incredible response I received from everyone who read it. *Mad Girl* was supposed to be 'an upbeat book about depression' but I absolutely hated writing it because it was so very hard to rake up all the painful things I had long tried to bury under a toxic tsunami of alcohol, drugs and terrible relationships. It was like sitting down at a desk every day to hack away at a nasty scab until it became a pus-filled open wound.

But I am so, so glad I did it. Since *Mad Girl* came out in June 2016, I have learnt more about myself than I had in the entire preceding ten years, and the reason I learnt so much about myself is because I learnt so much about the people who read it, who emailed me and came up to me in the street and shared their stories back with me. I was very clear that I did not want *Mad Girl* to be seen as a self-help book, on account of the fact that I have never been able to help myself; because I was not an expert in mental illness, just someone who had plenty of experience of it. I was aware of the fine line between sharing your story and trying to shape someone else's. I just wanted people to read *Mad Girl* and feel comforted; to know that they were not alone, despite what they felt. 'No miracle cure for mental illness is to be found in this book,' I wrote, back in the early winter of 2016. 'I cannot say that reading it will change your life or transform your wellbeing or any of the other frankly wild claims made by so many of the millions of self-help books out there on the market . . . So no, this is not a self-help book. It is just my story. My only hope is that by reading it, you might feel able to share yours, too.'

But this book? Well I suppose you could classify it as Sort-Of-Self-Help-Memoir. (Do you think that will catch on? Might I be able to pitch it to Waterstones?) It is Sort-Of-Self-Help-Memoir, inspired by all the ways readers have helped me – I suppose, then, Sort-Of-Self-Help-Memoir-Combined-With-The-Help-I-Received-Through-Meeting-Other-People. (Not so catchy, but more accurate.) Because I can honestly say that the biggest part of my recovery (whatever recovery is) has not been therapy or antidepressants or exercise, though they have all played a part. The biggest part of my recovery has been hearing your stories. It has been meeting people who look normal and learning that they, too, have intrusive thoughts about whether or not they've burnt the house down or become a mass murderer.

Lightbulb moments are rare, but they came in droves in the weeks after *Mad Girl* came out and I toured around the country promoting it, though promoting feels like such a shallow word given the profound encounters I had on that particular book tour. The mother who had lost her son to suicide and ended up in hospital herself; the seventeen-year-old girl who had been discharged from Accident and Emergency a day after an overdose attempt without any follow-up care in place; the 78-year-old woman who had never told a single soul about the crashing depressions she experienced ('I hope yours is the last generation that has to suffer in silence,' she said to me. 'Amen to that!' I wanted to shout, very loudly). I remember meeting a girl who told me she had the OCD that I had, the type that makes you think you might be a paedophile or a serial killer. She had short brunette hair, bright blue eyes, a lovely dress on from Topshop and a great handbag that she later told me was from Zara. 'YOU? A paedophile? Don't be so silly, you're clearly not!' I said. And it was only then that the penny dropped and I realised that I was thinking exactly what everyone else had thought when I told them about my horrible form of OCD.

It is because of that book and because of all those encounters and because of everything readers have told me that I have achieved the things I have in the last year or so. I am an ordinary human who just happens to have achieved some extraordinary things on account of the fact that I have been lucky enough to see – and be inspired by – the most incredible examples of the human spirit. Thanks to *Mad Girl*, I have met some of the most amazingly resilient people on the planet, people who have shown me that if you are going through hell, the best way to get through it is to keep going – and if you can find someone's hand to hold while you are doing that, then all the better. Knowing that there are other people out there who have experienced the same misery as me does not fill me with joy, but it does give me some sort of hope when the days get long and difficult, as they inevitably do. Every time I've wanted to give up and get back to writing about the travails of celebrities or the latest fashion craze, I think of the letters I receive and the people I have met and the friends I have made, and I keep on going. I think about what it felt like to suffer from a mental illness in silence and how awful that was, and how different things are now, and I get up and I go out. So I thought it was only fair to put all those things together in this book and pass them on to you.

Sometimes very lovely, kind people send me messages saying how brave and strong I am, and though these messages are clearly well-meaning, they do make me laugh. I have not fought in a war zone or stared down the barrel of a gun. I've done things literally anybody could do, if only they knew what the human spirit – what *their* human spirit – was capable of.

Do you think, on all the days I thought I was worthless and alone and a freak because that is what mental illness tells *everyone*, that I could have foreseen a time when I would be holding monthly picnics and walks for other people just like me, picnics and walks where we laughed and joked and had fun? That these monthly picnics and walks would eventually be held all over the country and in other countries, too?

Eat, Drink, Run.

And do you think that two years ago, when I was in the midst of a breakdown and my psychiatrist was suggesting I become an inpatient at a hospital, when I was shovelling back anti-psychotics as if they were Smarties just to get through the day, that I could have imagined I would – just a year later – end up being the person Prince Harry decided to talk to about his mental health? Me, the girl who can't leave the house some days, sitting on a sofa in Kensington Palace drinking tea with the coolest royal that ever was?

Do you think that just eighteen months ago, when I was hugely overweight and could barely run for a bus, that I pictured myself completing a marathon? An actual fucking marathon. Me! Twenty-six point two miles! Without having to give up booze and fags! (Though obviously I gave them up for the duration of the *actual* marathon.)

I wanted to write this book for the girl that I used to be. The one who had dreams but no realistic hopes of ever fulfilling them. The girl I meet and speak to every day, be it on the street or at book signings or on Instagram, the girl who sends me a message to say that she went out for a jog today because she saw that I did and if I did then it was definitely something she could at the very least try. The girl who has no idea of the power she holds, of the energy within her, of all the things she is more than capable of doing, because society has told her otherwise. Because society has told her that if she wants to do this then she has to look like that, and if she feels like achieving so and so she better be wearing the same outfit as What's-Her-Gob. This may, on the surface, seem like a book about a fat girl who got less fat and learned to be fit, but really it is a book about what you can do when you put your mind to things. It's a book that says 'If *I* can do a marathon, then anyone can. You can do whatever you damn well fancy. You can climb Everest if that's your bag (though don't mind me if I admire your progress from the sofa).'

So yes, I am a runner. I am a drinker, a smoker, an eater of burgers and chips, but a runner all the same. I always was a runner – the only person stopping me from getting out and doing it 'properly' was myself. While you read this book, I'm not going to ask you to do anything more strenuous than sit still or – ideally – lie flat (on a very comfortable sofa, or perhaps even a Lazy Boy) and keep an open mind. Actually, I am going to ask you to do a couple of tiny things – but don't worry, you won't have to move. Firstly, think not of what you aren't, but what you are. Secondly, remember that one day, things could happen to you that you wouldn't be able to believe right now – the most astonishing, amazing things. Trust me when I say that all you have to do is hold on.

1

To the Park

Someone once told me that I treated my body like an amusement park. The person in question was a beautiful colleague I sat next to who didn't really drink alcohol or eat carbs; she was basically the polar opposite of me, and everything about us showed this. While she was always on time for work, I was always late. While she would arrive with fascinating tales of cultural outings she had been on with her boyfriend the night before, I would arrive with tales of waking up in a stranger's house and having to stop off at Topshop on the way in to buy a new pair of knickers and tights.

She did things like get blow-dries, and manicures; I was not against these as such but I could usually only be bothered to book in for them once somebody had staged an intervention and warned me that I was 'beginning to look a bit trampy'. I took this as a compliment, you know. I thought it showed just the right amount of insouciance: a casual indifference to my appearance because I was, I dunno, deep or something. Of course, it was the opposite, really, a stunning, or not-so-stunning result of deep-rooted insecurity that could be seen in the amount of alcohol I was drinking and the quantity of drugs I was taking, but I was in denial and didn't want to see it that way. I was carefree! I wasn't going to be taken in by all that 'looking good' shit, that was surely just a result of oppression from the patriarchy! So deep in madness was I, it never occurred to me that my friend was just, you know, *looking after herself*. Being kind to herself. Displaying elements of self-care.

'You treat your body like an amusement park,' she said that particular lunch time. She was right. I must have been twenty-eight, twenty-nine. I was having an affair with a married man and taking significantly more cocaine than one should take, which is none at all. I ate five packets of crisps a day which I would occasionally throw up – I had had bulimia since the age of nineteen, because wasn't that just what people had? The only time I raised my heart rate was when I snorted a line of cocaine – the last proper exercise I had done was at secondary school, when I had played netball and rounders before growing boobs and realising that frenetic movement was painful.

I was probably eating one of the bags of crisps when she made the amusement park comment. Quavers, I imagine. I loved Quavers. It was like ingesting cheesy air. Anyway, I wasn't put out by her comparing me to, say, Alton Towers or Chessington World of Adventures or Thorpe Park – although I suspect that I was more likely to be one of those crap amusement parks, the kind you find in dilapidated, depressed seaside towns that had their heyday back in the eighties but everyone has long since stopped going to. I agreed with her entirely, and actually saw it as a good thing. 'It's so much fun!' I replied, probably opening another bag of crisps, though who honestly remembers given that all of my twenties blur into one long hangover?

I can now see that having fun is not the same as being happy. But back then I couldn't. I was also blissfully unaware that treating your body like an amusement park, rather than a body, was not a healthy way to live. You can't ride the roller coaster every day and expect to feel sane. You can't live on candyfloss and expect to feel good. Was that why amusement parks shut down for certain parts of the year? The rides need maintenance, so that they don't break down. Everything needs a lick of paint, so it doesn't look tired. Ice cream tastes good in the baking summer but not so great in the deep midwinter.

Living like this may have been fun, but it was in no way sustainable. Eventually, everything was going to have to grind to a halt. And so it was with my body, year after year, me behaving like an over-excited child who would eventually end up having a breakdown, until one year I somehow managed to produce a child of my own and it became clear that I was going to have to grow up. That I was going to have to start treating my body like a body.

From a very young age, my life had felt like a bit of a roller coaster. It wasn't that I had a miserable childhood, or an unsupportive family. It was just that I was scared the whole time. Ridiculously, overwhelmingly scared, like I was on a loop-the-loop or a log flume. As a small child I was worried about nuclear war. I became convinced the house was going to burn down. I wouldn't let my siblings hang their Christmas stockings inside – they had to be put on the front door – because I didn't like the idea of a strange, bearded man creeping into our bedroom. At twelve, I developed OCD. I became convinced that I was dying of AIDS, and later that I might be a serial killer who had blanked out all the grisly details of the murders in shock. People who have read my last book, *Mad Girl*, will know about this, so I won't go into massive detail – I want this to be an uplifting read, not one that makes you wish you had just sat down with a nice magazine instead. By the age of nineteen my hair had fallen out and I looked like Donald Trump with a combover. The bulimia came after, as did the booze and the drugs, but I really thought I was winning at life. I had managed to get a career in journalism and mentally ill people didn't do that, did they? They rocked back and forth in padded cells, or so I had learnt from most of the media portrayals I had seen of people with mental illness. In time, I came to see my funny little turns as something that just happened to me from time to time, like a cold sore or tonsilitis.

At the age of thirty-one, I met Harry. Harry also worked at the *Telegraph* and was everything that my previous paramours, if you could even call them that, hadn't been. He was kind, loyal and trustworthy. At first I ignored him because he seemed to me kind of ordinary, though in time I would come to see him as extraordinary. He didn't seem to mind my little foibles. We were living together within four months, I was pregnant within a further ten, and almost two years after we shared our first kiss we welcomed our baby daughter Edie, getting married three months later.

I put on a lot of weight during this time; once more I was treating my body like an amusement park, just in a different way. I wasn't on the roller coaster now; I was on the kiddy rides, scoffing back as much food as I could, enjoying the view, because I was a mum now and I was not going to be defined by my body shape. I was going to be defined by my *personality*! I got really fat during this time. Just over sixteen stone.

19

I mean, fat enough that the only way I could wear Zara or Topshop was if I bought a belt and wore it as a necklace, or styled out a thong as a hairband. Fat enough that I weighed more than my husband. Fat enough that thin people stopped moaning about how fat they were in my presence (a surefire way of knowing you've piled on the pounds). Fat enough that people had long ago stopped mistaking me for being pregnant, on account of the fact that my belly was perfectly in sync with the flab on the rest of my body. Fat enough to piss off Katie Hopkins, who once wrote a column about my size (this, I thought, was well worth tucking into the Domino's for). Fat enough that the odd *Telegraph* reader started to write to me to tell me how fat I was, and how I was surely about to die a terrible death from diabetes or heart failure. I found their concern touching, but felt compelled to reply that they really didn't need to worry. I was fine. I felt way healthier mentally than I had when I was bulimic, and existing only on Quavers, cigarettes, vodka, cocaine and thin air.

I thought I was cured – my weight was surely a sign of my mental wellness. I thought motherhood would do for me what an intensive course of psychotherapy does for everyone else. With Harry and Edie there would be no more chaos, no more madness. And for a while, it worked. For a while, I got away with it. I tricked people into thinking I was fixed, because I appeared to have taken to parenting like a duck to water. While other new mums seemed to be struggling with the sleepless nights, I was finding them kind of relaxing. Waking up all night with a baby was way better than staying up all night on cocaine. Plus, I was used to the elevated hygiene levels that came with a newborn. I had been living them since the age of twelve – sterilising bottles really felt like nothing new to me. I had the husband, the baby, the flat, the brand new Bugaboo. I was living the dream. I wrote a book about my crazy twenties called *The Wrong Knickers*. It did quite well. The film rights were sold. Everywhere I went, people congratulated me on turning my life around. I did too. Screw you, OCD, I would exclaim! Screw you! I have beaten you, finally.

Of course, it came back then, worse than ever, having crept in on a stealth mission over many months while I had been working too hard and trying to be The Perfect Mother™. This time, my OCD told me that I might have hurt my own child. My dearest, darling child, my life force, literally my own flesh and blood, and my OCD had me wondering whether or not I had molested her and somehow forgotten about it. Right now, you might be thinking, 'But if you knew it was OCD, why didn't you just IGNORE IT?' That is the cunning of the illness, which is also known as the 'doubting disease'. It makes you think you don't have it, that this time you really *have* done something absolutely terrible.

21

Eat, Drink, Run.

So I couldn't hug my child. When I looked at her the love I felt was overwhelmed by the fear that I had done something terrible to her. Changing nappies became almost an impossibility. I would sit by her cot at night watching her breathing so I could be sure she was still alive. But I was never sure, not really. I would try to leave and my brain would suggest I might have strangled her; I would have to sit back down to check that her tiny, beautiful chest was moving up and down. In time, my husband set up a camp bed next to Edie's cot and slept there instead so I could have a proper night's rest in our room, without fretting. It was then that I realised that I was allowing my OCD to take over not just my life, but that of my husband and child.

And I was damned if I was going to let that happen. I was damned if I was going to allow my daughter to grow up with the same misery as I did, damned if I was going to let her live in a world where people with mental illnesses felt that they had to suffer in silence. So I did the only thing I knew: I wrote about it, in my *Telegraph* column. Writing about it was frightening, sure – how *do* you explain in a light and upbeat manner that you have an illness that makes you think you might be a serial-killing paedophile? – but it felt completely necessary. It was a way of putting OCD in its place, a way of showing it who was boss. I even gave it a name, Jareth the Goblin King, after the evil but ever-so-slightly alluring David Bowie character in the eighties movie *Labyrinth*. I felt I was gaining power over Jareth for the first time. I had no idea quite what I was starting, how my life was about to head off in a completely new direction, changing things for the better forever more.

What happened next still has the power to take my breath away, in the best way possible. The column came out on a Sunday in January 2015, and by midday I had received almost a hundred emails from readers telling me that I was not alone, that they had experienced the misery of mental illness too – if not OCD, then something else. Over the next few weeks I received many more hundreds of emails, cards and letters from people telling me their stories. I was beginning to realise that feeling weird is really, really normal . . . that in fact, the people who claim to be normal the whole time were the real freaks. Speaking up, writing about my OCD, had blown a hole in its most powerful weapon: silence. I was coming to see that what all mental illness has in common is its ability to lie to people, to tell us that we are freaks, that nobody else will understand what we are going through. Once you expose it for what it is – an illness like any other – you are well on the way to finding the magic solution that you have failed to find through drugs and alcohol and staying quiet. It was empowering. It was more than that. It was life-changing.

Eat, Drink, Run.

My publishers had originally wanted me to write a novel next, something light and fluffy in a similar vein to *The Wrong Knickers*, only fictional. Then they saw the response my columns were getting, and they changed tack. I remember my agent and editor taking me out for coffee one cold February morning. 'We were thinking you should write a memoir about your mental health,' they announced. 'A sort of light-hearted book about depression!' Oh yeah, sure!

And so the idea for *Mad Girl* was born, an idea I steadfastly ignored for most of the year because I was feeling OK and had absolutely no desire to delve into the darkness I was beginning to leave behind. Also, I am disorganised. I have never written anything without the threat of a deadline hanging over me. As winter set in during 2015, I began to write, and it suddenly seemed like writing this book was the thing that was going to finish me off forever. By the time I was 50,000 words in, I was on my knees, a wreck of a human who had already missed two deadlines. I was in the house day and night, leaving only to take my daughter to nursery, hoping that I might be run over on the way home. Being run over became a fantasy of mine – I thought that the physical pain would be so unbearable that it would at least take away the emotional pain. I turned up to a book meeting in floods of tears, and was sent home. The editor of the *Telegraph* called me into his office and told me to take some time off. Do you know how much of a mess you have to be for a newspaper editor to tell you to take a break? You basically have to be falling apart.

Unbeknownst to me, my agent and book editor were busy having a series of high-level meetings in which the possibility of pulling *Mad Girl* was seriously discussed. They felt that asking me to write about my illness had turned out to be a serious dereliction of duty, and that they couldn't allow my wellbeing to be sacrificed at the altar of book sales. They came to my flat to tell me this, to inform me that I didn't have to write another word and that I could forget about paying them back the advance, and something inside me just flipped. I was not going to let Jareth beat me. I was not going to let Jareth win. 'I am going to finish this book,' I told them. 'I am going to finish this book if it's the last thing I do.' And they looked a little ashen-faced before my agent said: 'Yeah, that's kind of what we're worried about.'

I sent them on their way. For my child, I was going to get through this.

So there I was, in a very dark place, with 20,000 words of the book still to go and nothing left inside me but stone cold determination, when I remembered something else that amusement-park girl had once said to me. 'Sometimes, half the battle is getting out the house,' she said. She meant well, I know. By this point she could see that I wasn't well, and she was only trying to help. But it irritated me. What did she know about the battle of leaving her perfect house, its front door probably painted in Farrow and Ball? When she said it, I remember looking down at the clothes on my body and the shoes on my feet and being astonished by the very fact that I had actually managed to get dressed at all. Leaving the house wasn't half the battle. It *was* the battle.

To say that leaving the house is half the battle is to seriously undermine the battle. It's like announcing that the Mongols conquering nearly all of continental Asia and the Middle East was just a load of people making a mountain out of a molehill. It's like saying that Stalingrad was nothing more than a storm in a teacup. Try telling *that* to the several million people whose lives and homes were destroyed by the Germans. And so it is with mental health. Leaving the house may seem to the average well person like a whole lot of fuss being made out of nothing. But when you're in the depths of depression, when you are being attacked by anxiety, simply getting out of bed can seem like travelling to the moon. Getting to the corner shop can feel like climbing Everest.

If they say that the average person spends a third of their life asleep in bed, then I have probably spent another third awake in bed, wallowing in my own sweat and self-loathing, unable to get upright. You know how people often call depression the Black Dog? Well, I don't. I don't, because in my mind dogs are jumpy and frenetic and always want to be walked, and when they're not always wanting to be walked they are sleeping peacefully at the feet of their loving owner. For me, mental illness isn't anything like that. It's more like being crushed under the weight of an eighteen-tonne Black Elephant, or clinging onto the back of a Black Sloth, hoping desperately that I'm not going to fall off into the deep dark jungle below. Do you know what I suffer from? The Black Slug. I'm thinking of getting one tattooed on my wrist. 'What's that?' people will ask curiously about the splodge of ink just below my left hand. 'It's my Black Slug,' I will reply, wisely. 'It signifies how I feel when I am swallowed by the vast and lonely chasm of depression.' And then I will nod in a grave and serious manner as they slowly back the fuck away and vow never to invite me to a dinner party again.

Good. I don't like dinner parties anyway. Too much focus on the food, not enough on the wine.

So yeah, getting up and out of the house hasn't always come easily to me. In fact, it still doesn't. You know how some people have to factor in an extra half an hour in the morning to blow-dry their hair? Well, I use that time to have an exhausting internal dialogue about the relative merits of getting out of bed. I know, I know – getting out of bed will do me good. And yet! The eighteen-tonne Black Elephant is totally sitting on my chest, and it's freaking both me and my husband out. I don't know what the eighteen-tonne Black Elephant ate for dinner last night or if it bothered to brush its teeth afterwards, but it has fucking awful morning breath, the type that pins you to the pillow in horror. And sometimes I feel that just getting the creature off my chest is going to require the help of a crane, to winch it out the bedroom window.

Those times, I have no idea how I have managed to get up and go to the office. Not a clue. And when I get there, I half expect to be greeted with dancing girls, someone jumping out of a cake, and an aeroplane writing things in the sky. 'LOOK!' I want to shout. 'I LEFT THE HOUSE!'

Sometimes, it amazes me that I am still alive. That I didn't fall off the roller coaster, or drown in the waters around the log flume, or disappear in the ghost train.

But maybe amusement-park girl had a point. I had read somewhere – in many places, actually – that exercise helped with mental health issues. I had read it, but for a long time, about two decades in fact, I had not wanted to believe it. I had wanted to be the first person to prove that actually, drinking all the booze and taking all the cocaine helped with mental health issues. 'Guys, guys!' I would shout, my Eureka! moment realised. 'I have found the perfect way to get fucked up without actually fucking yourself up!'

I tried and I tried but even I could see that this

strategy didn't seem to be working for me. Worse, it seemed to be making me . . . well, worse. I thought: maybe my slim, happy, healthy-looking friend who eats kale and goes to spin classes is actually on to something. Maybe she is right to be concerned about my whole amusement-park approach to life. Maybe these so-called experts actually know what they are talking about. Maybe I should listen to their knowledge, experience and scientific wisdom and accept that perhaps, just *perhaps*, they know better than me, a girl whose only scientific qualification is a B in Chemistry GCSE. I thought: let's just give this a try. God loves a tryer, even if I don't believe in God, because if God existed there would be no war or famine or pestilence or OCD. And in the end, it wasn't as if I had a choice. It wasn't as if I had anything left in my armoury. The drugs weren't working any more – not even the prescribed ones. Even the writing, the thing I thought I would always be able to do, had left me. The only other option I could see, other than going outside and attempting to release endorphins through exercise, was to stay in the flat feeding the eighteen-tonne Black Elephant until eventually it would squash and suffocate me. I didn't fancy that. I may have had a mental illness that from time to time told me I was the worst human in the world, but somewhere in my brain there was something that wanted to prove otherwise. There was nothing for it. I was going to have to move.

Eat, Drink, Run.

And what was the worst that could happen, really? If I didn't like moving, I could just come home and climb back into my cave. The bed would still be there, the sheets and pillows still in a crumpled heap. It wasn't as if taking positive action was going to magically make it all disappear. I would be like a small child trying broccoli for the first time – worst case scenario, I would spit it out in disgust; best case, I would find a delicious *and* nutritious thing that could help me to live a happier, healthier life.

The only real problem I had was a lack of 'athleisurewear', those skin-tight, Lycra outfits that I had admired on many mums at nursery drop-off, in much the same way one admires the Crown Jewels – lovely and all that, but not something I'm ever going to get my hands on. I had heard of brands such as 'LuluLemon' and 'Sweaty Betty' but they were no more familiar to me than haute couture. So I had to improvise. I found a pair of tracksuit bottoms that felt remarkably tight around the thigh; my inner critic – Jareth, perhaps – loomed large and said to me, 'Only you could take an item meant to be baggy and make them look like leggings, you great big fatty.' Then I pulled a T-shirt out of my husband's drawer – it was a *Star Wars* one, but by this point, what did I care? I was hardly getting dressed up for a posh do. I didn't own anything like a sports bra, but figured that my 36JJ boobs already required lingerie that was actually scaffolding, and that would probably work. The one big obstacle to my burgeoning running career was a lack of running shoes. Even I knew that you couldn't jog in ballet pumps or slippers. I found a pair of leopard-print Converse that had holes in the heel and decided that they would have to do. When you're desperate, you'll take anything.

As I stepped out the door that cold January morning, I was aware that I must have looked like a woman on day release from a mental institution, the mental institution being my own head. I had a long way to go before I matched the immaculate levels of my colleague. But I didn't care. When you are in immense pain, you find it difficult to give much of a toss about anything other than alleviating said pain – it's why women in labour don't much care when their bowels are released during the big push. Just get this thing out of me. I literally do not give a shit about anything else.

I took a deep breath and started putting one foot in front of the other at a slightly faster speed than normal – when I say fast, I of course don't actually mean fast. I got about fifty metres down the street before I became convinced I was dying. Water. I. Just. Needed. Water. I turned back and went to the flat to retrieve a bottle of Evian or something similar. We didn't have any, of course – we are the kind of family who drink straight out of the tap. Clutching at straws – literally – I found a pink plastic beaker that belonged to my daughter. I filled it, and went back on my way.

Eat, Drink, Run.

I was a woman on a mission – a woman in a *Star Wars* T-shirt and leopard-print Converse clutching a Tommy Tippee cup. What did I think I was going to do? Complete a marathon? Ha!

I must have been out there for no more than twenty minutes. But it was twenty minutes not sat inside in my own head. It was not pleasant, I'll readily admit that. My lungs felt like they were on fire, sweat poured into every roll of fat and flab, and my face looked as if it had just been exposed to the glare of a nuclear bomb. But . . . it wasn't as unpleasant as being crushed under the weight of slugs, sloths and elephants. When I moved I was OK, even if I wasn't. I was just trying to stay alive. Actually, there's no 'just' about it. I WAS trying to stay alive, and that in itself sent a message of hope to my body. When I moved, when I felt my flab jig jollily up and down, I was at a very basic level acknowledging that the world was still spinning, even if Jareth was doing his level best to give me every impression to the contrary. And I realised, while I was out there, that depression *wants* to keep you in your own house, preferably in your own bed, because if you stay there, you stay in your own head. There is no chance of distraction or deviation from the many lies that a mental illness has the capacity to tell you. You'd be amazed at all the ways you can believe the world could end without you needing to actually leave the house . . . or maybe you wouldn't. You're reading this book; probably you are well aware of the tricks a mental illness will play on you, the tales that it will tell. And that's what all mental illness has in common: it lies to you. It tells you that you are a freak. It tells you that nobody will ever understand how you are feeling. It tells you that you are alone. Out on that jog, I had my first inkling that all was not as it seemed.

The next day, every limb and muscle in my body ached. It was terrible. But it was no more terrible than the stuff that had been going through my head the day before. It was just physical pain, and I could do that. Two days later, I went out again. And as I continued to do that, I started to be able to write again. I found I wasn't fantasising quite so much about being knocked down by a car. I didn't realise it, but I was getting better.

Saturday, 30 January 2016. *Mad Girl* is due out in precisely five months. It is not done, but the finish line is within sight. I am running every other day not out of desire or enjoyment but necessity. By this point I have bought a pair of cheap trainers and a bigger pair of tracksuit bottoms but I am still rocking the *Star Wars* T-shirt. This particular morning, I set out for my 'run' – really, more of a shuffle, hop and a step – and decide that I am not going to listen to Take That and Taylor Swift. I am trying to improve my body and my mind, so Radio 4 it is. There is a documentary on that is presented by Jarvis Cocker. This makes me feel cool, even if the *Star Wars* T-shirt suggests otherwise. It is a documentary about the author Carson McCullers, whose first novel, *The Heart Is a Lonely Hunter*, was all about the isolation felt by a group of American outcasts. I listen intently, as guests tell Cocker about how exquisitely and painfully McCullers captured what it is like to be a teenager. I learn that McCullers was a depressive who tried to kill herself. She was also an alcoholic who died in 1967 at the age of just fifty.

The documentary ends with some archive audio footage of McCullers. 'All people belong to a "We" except me,' says a voice from the past speaking to me today. I am so taken by what she says, so moved by it, that I find myself slipping in some mud. I catch myself talking out loud – always a good sign. 'You were wrong, Carson,' I say. 'You were wrong. You belonged to a "We"; you just didn't know it.' A speedy man in smart Lycra pants shoots me a look, but I couldn't give a toss. I get up, dust myself down (or mud myself down?) and look around me. I look at the houses around the common, some of which almost inevitably contain people who have suffered from mental illness. I look at the top deck of a bus that drives by, and surmise that the number 37 is also probably transporting a couple of Carson's We. I even look for the speedy man in Lycra and chastise myself for being so judgemental of him – who is to say he wasn't running away from some problems, too? Come back, man in Lycra, come back, all is forgiven!

I run home, and resolve to find Carson's We.

At home, I find Harry playing dolls with Edie. I am as animated as either has seen me in several months; I feel a bit like a fizzy drink can shaken up, only it isn't Coke bubbling up to the surface now but all the misery and anxiety I have carried around for so bloody long.

'I'm wondering,' I say to Harry, 'why there aren't any groups for people like me. And why, if I want to meet other people who have an illness that sometimes tells them they are a serial-killing paedophile, I have to go to a psychiatric hospital, even though we know that one in four of us will suffer from a mental health issue each year so actually we are pretty common and, dare I say it, NORMAL. I'm out there this morning, looking at groups of mums pushing buggies together, groups of men playing football together, groups of weirdos being beasted by men dressed in pretend army fatigues, also together, and I'm thinking, WHY CAN'T I COME TOGETHER OUTSIDE WITH *MY* PEOPLE? WHY IS THERE NOTHING FOR US?'

Harry stays very quiet.

'I'm thinking, what if I create a group for people who have mental health issues, one where people have an actual *reason* to get outside, that reason being getting to meet like-minded souls and do a bit of exercise, even if that exercise is just walking around the park? It could be lovely!'

'It could be a disaster,' he finally says.

'You're so negative!'

'But what if a load of nutters turn up?'

'That's the point, Harry. THAT'S THE WHOLE BLOODY POINT! I want nutters to turn up! The nuttier, the better! I want all of us to come together so we can prove to the world that actually, it's perfectly normal to feel nutty.'

'You're mad,' he says, returning to Edie's dolls.

'And that is a surprise to you how, exactly?'

The first Mental Health Mates (MHM) takes place on Sunday, 14 February 2016 in Hyde Park, London. I choose Valentine's Day because I think that is a day that most people find pretty miserable, even the chronically coupled up, on account of the fact that nobody can ever live up to a greeting card notion of love. (Sounds deep, huh?) I tweet out my brainwave the day I have it, and am pleased to see fifty-three retweets. Fifty-three! I know it's not Brooklyn Beckham territory – a man who can post a picture of a spoon and garner three billion likes – but it's a start. I try to feel gratitude for the twenty-seven people who have favourited it, but am instead eaten up by an irrational sense of resentment towards them. Please, don't just LIKE my tweet. Just LIKING my tweet is nice, but it's not ENOUGH. It's basically your way of saying, 'I get what you're trying to do here, but I am not going to get behind it and actually put it on my timeline in case you end up setting up some sort of freaky cult like the Moonies and I am later held accountable for it.' Oh man, my ability to see the bad in everything makes me feel so . . . well, *bad*.

My friend Chloe tells me she is coming with me because, as she says, 'Having seen the worst of you for so long, I really can't wait to see the best.' Chloe is very arch. You have to be to deal with me. All my friends, I am realising, have a very high tolerance – for alcohol, for bad behaviour, for my endless fucking capacity to make a tit out of myself. Chloe has watched me fall over drunk, vomit into a handbag, and one time she made me go to work dressed in sequins after an all-night bender because she said it would bring out the sparkle in my eyes. I realise now that she was playing a trick on me. But then she also used to let me crash at her flat during lunch break (we worked together) if I had gone out on an all-night bender and not had any sleep. That was kind. When I got together with Harry, she spent quite a lot of time saying 'poor Harry, poor Harry' over and over again, but in reality I think she was relieved that someone else had taken me off her hands. Still, the speed at which I got into the whole couple thing took her by surprise – looking back, I think it took *me* by surprise. When I had Edie, she came round with a bottle of champagne and a packet of Marlboro Reds – she thought I would appreciate the biggest head rush possible after so long off the gaspers. But I like to think that she is genuinely intrigued today. Perhaps she even likes the idea of a place where she can go and feel normal. I'm even starting to believe that maybe, just maybe, in her dry way, she actually wants to support me in my endeavour. 'Thanks for coming,' I say, anticipating her moving speech about how proud she is of me for doing something *good* for once. 'I'm single,' she replies. 'It's Valentine's Day. What else was I going to do?'

Leaving my husband and child in the warm, toasty flat to venture out with my psychotic best friend, it does occur to me that I might have finally taken leave of all of my senses. Outside the wind is howling and it has started to rain. The sky is slate grey. Who on earth is going to come and meet me in a freezing park in central London on the most miserable day of the year? If you had a predilection for misery, and found it difficult to haul yourself out of the house most days of the week, why on earth would you suddenly decide it seems like a good idea today?

I put this to Chloe as we walk towards the café in Hyde Park, my heart hammering in my chest. For once, she agrees with me. 'I mean, you'd have to be seriously loopy to think it's a good idea to come here off the back of a tweet from a stranger. Completely mad. Either that or desperate, I suppose. The only reason I am here is because you're my friend and I feel sorry for you. Also, because as much as I take the piss out of you, I don't want you to be killed by a lunatic off the internet. Most people on the internet are lunatics, really. Either they were already a lunatic, or they are turned into one by petty Twitter squabbles between the left and the right about the Tories. You stare at social media for long enough, and you will go completely and utterly bonkers. I've seen it happen. I know someone who became so addicted to the Valencia filter on Instagram that she got a make-up artist to come up with a special look that mimics the essential warmth of its tone.'

I glare at Chloe. For once it is me losing patience with her. 'Chloe, I know that I have made it very, very hard for anyone to take me in the slightest bit seriously. I am conscious that the last three decades of my life have been a bit of a joke. But I'm trying to do something IMPORTANT here. And as I have never tried to do anything important in my life, it would be great if you could give me some back-up. My whole *raison d'être*, for the last thirty-four and a half years, has been to be as frivolous and fluffy as possible, because if I am frivolous and fluffy then I never have to confront the dense, dark stuff that I have somehow managed to bury deep in my head. But that dense, dark stuff is beginning to bubble up. It's starting to bubble over. And if I'm not careful, it will bubble all over the frivolous and fluffy life I have carefully created for myself and ruin it FOR EVER. Would you please, just for today, pretend to be an open-minded citizen of the world even if you think what I'm doing is all a load of bollocks?'

'Bryony,' says Chloe, smiling at me. 'Look over there.' She motions to a table outside the café, where twenty or so people are huddled together for warmth, half waving at me. I almost feel like fainting in shock. Instead I grin wildly, wave back, and then run to the public toilet next door where I have a little cry.

Once, when I was a little girl, my grandfather told me about the word numinous. Petee was a committed atheist and often joked that if either of us walked into a church we would most likely burst into flames (something I am still convinced is true, causing me to wear only flame-retardant outfits whenever I have to attend a wedding, christening or carol concert). But that wasn't to say that he didn't believe in miracles, or magic. He had a strong sense of the universe, he told me, a strong sense of things that felt *numinous*. I was eight. I had no idea what he was chatting about. Probably I thought he was having a funny turn, that maybe we needed to take him to hospital. I may even have shouted: 'Mum!

Grandad's blathering on again, I think it's time for him to take his pills.' I was that kind of child: obnoxious, as well as anxious – a terrible combination. Anyway, there he was, trying to explain the concept of higher powers and spiritual awakenings, when all I was really interested in was whether or not my little sister had nicked my favourite Polly Pocket. Something that was numinous, explained my patient grandfather, was something that had a divine quality to it, something that felt special, almost magic. 'Like Paul Daniels?' I said. Petee shook his head and that was the end of that.

Twenty-five years later, outside that café, I was beginning to understand the meaning of the word numinous. Whatever it was – something spiritual, something divine, something that had the power to send shivers down your spine – I felt it that day in the park. I stood in front of Chloe, sweet, cynical Chloe, and all of those people I had never met before, and I announced to them that I had an illness that sometimes made me think I had molested a child or killed people. It was the first time I had actually said the words out loud, in front of anyone. Sure, I had written the words, I had thought the words, I had hmmed and ahhed and tried to explain the words in a roundabout way to therapists and doctors and, very occasionally, my mum. But I had never said them clearly, loudly, for myself before. Yet having all those people standing in front of me, all of those people who had come to the park not in spite of their mental health but *because* of it . . . well, I finally felt the freedom to be really, properly truthful. I felt free for the first time. There, in the wind, I wasn't scared any more. I was not a freak. I was just me. And now I was starting to amass an army that would help me fight Jareth, that would help us fight all of our versions of Jareth.

'Who here has taken or takes antidepressants?' I asked. An elderly couple sheltering under an umbrella nearby looked taken aback, and shuffled away. Slowly but surely, people started to put their hands up, including – to my surprise – Chloe. I was astonished. Here was my best friend, a woman I thought I knew inside out, and yet I hadn't a clue that she had taken Citalopram for six months just the year before. How many more of us were out there, I wondered? How many more of us were spending our lives pretending to be OK? And was it actually OK not to be OK? Were we all terrified of showing each other our dark sides without realising that almost everyone else has them too? Were we all suffering in silence completely unnecessarily? It seemed clear to me that the answer to that question was a resounding yes.

Seeing all these seemingly normal people, people who I previously would have passed in the street and assumed to be the kind of folk who had it all sorted – when in fact some of them had attempted suicide and others had been sectioned – was mind-blowing to me. It was mind-blowing and it was strangely empowering. For the very first time in my life, I knew in my gut that I wasn't mad. These were not the head-clutchers you always saw in newspapers and magazines, though I was sure that we all had done some serious head-clutching in our time. These were not the mentally ill as depicted in the movies – freaks or outcasts rocking back and forth and screeching in a padded cell, though I am sure we had all *felt* a bit like that at some point or other. These were normal people with families and jobs and friends who simply happened to have experienced mental health issues. They shopped in Topshop and watched Netflix and liked to get a daily coffee from Starbucks or Pret. They supported football teams, spent too much time on Instagram, listened to Madonna. They were indistinguishable from normal people, because they were normal people. Here, for the first time, I had the sense that together, we were shining a light on something that had previously been left in the dark: the fact that mental illness is an illness like any other.

While writing this chapter, I wanted to give these people voices. I wanted to give them voices because I didn't want you to have to take my word for it. I wanted you to be able to see for yourselves that the people who responded to my tweet may have been desperate, but they were not in any way unusual or weird. They weren't, in the words of Chloe, loopy or completely bonkers, not by anybody's definition of the words. They had issues, sure, but who doesn't? So, for a moment, I'm going to hand over to them . . .

Denean

Something wasn't quite right. I had days where I would feel incredibly sad for no reason. Days where I would worry about things that I couldn't possibly have control over and days where I felt incredibly lonely. But when I saw Bryony's tweet about a walk and a cup of tea (or coffee in my case) in Hyde Park on Valentine's Day, for people with mental health issues, I thought it would be a good idea to go because it might help me stop feeling alone and maybe I might find out how to get the help that I knew, deep down, I needed. And I don't regret it for a second. It changed my life for the better.

Denean's Black Dog: Mine would be a snake. The sly way that judgemental and mean thoughts slither into my head and stop me from doing things, makes me think of a snake. Also, snakes are gross.

Neil

I had an anxiety and panic disorder breakdown in the summer of 2015. This was for a variety of reasons and it had been many years in the making.

By January 2016 I had used up my six NHS CBT sessions and finished a four-week Saturday morning meditation course in Covent Garden. I now didn't have anything in place to help my recovery, which felt daunting, but then I saw a tweet from Bryony asking if anyone wanted to meet up for a mental health version of Alcoholics Anonymous. I knew I needed to find something and it would be good to talk to others who had experienced similar difficulties – I had not really met anyone else who had struggled with the issues I was having. Emails were exchanged and the meet-up was set for Hyde Park on 14 February, Valentine's Day. I then had to say to my partner, 'Erm, would you mind me meeting up with a *Telegraph* journalist on Valentine's Day with other people who are all suffering from mental health issues?' Thankfully she is very understanding.

The 14 February date came around. I was apprehensive, having to fight off the voice that says you don't have to go, or what if you are the only one that turns up – the usual self-doubt and self-sabotage – but there was something inside telling me this was the right thing to do and I knew I had to go and I would regret it if I didn't.

The first meeting was supposed to involve some jogging, so I bought some running tights. I'm normally a jeans guy so wearing these things on the tube made me pretty self-conscious but I did end up doing a little running that day as I got my cafés mixed up so I had to run to the correct one. When I arrived, out of breath, dishevelled and dressed in black like I was attending a fitness funeral, I could not quite believe that there were about twenty others there and I wasn't the only man. We all sat around and drank hot drinks, then had a walk around the Serpentine. I still smile now when I think back to that February morning when twenty-odd strangers met up in Hyde Park and how what I thought would be a one-off meeting turned into a regular event. I have met and made friends with the most amazing group of people, who are determined to persevere against their difficulties. I am at most of the Hyde Park meet-ups, have been to a few pubs, been to museums. I brought along my partner and daughter to meet the group, all normal stuff, with normal people, talking about normal things.

Mental Health Mates celebrated its first birthday this year with old and new mates and I couldn't help but notice and admire the progress that people had made in their lives over that year. I look forward to the meet-ups and always feel better for going. Good things happen when you try new things and move out of your comfort zone.

Neil's Black Dog: A crocodile – hiding under the surface, it's menacing and attacks with little notice. It only has one thing on its mind – to take you.

Imogen

I'd been home from university for about six months. I hadn't wanted to come home – I desperately wanted to stay, had a provisional place on a year-long extension course in Management, but missed my grades. Graduating felt like stepping into an abyss – I didn't have anything lined up jobwise, I was going to have to move back in with my parents – at least, I thought, I can work on my mental health. But it got worse. I had no structure, I was being rejected by jobs – even by unpaid internships – left, right and centre. I'd gone from being able to text any one of my friends and be in their room drinking tea within twenty minutes to having no one around me. All of my friends were either still at university doing masters degrees or off travelling the world and I was completely stranded. And probably the most pervasive 'echo chamber' I had at university was a positive attitude towards mental health. I know almost no one who studied the arts or humanities at a high-achieving university who didn't have

47

mental health issues of some sort so everyone was incredibly open and understanding. I was exceptionally lucky not to meet anyone there who seriously believed depressed people should just cheer up and stop feeling sorry for themselves, or who thought that someone in the throes of a panic attack should just calm down.

Suddenly, back home, I was being told not to talk about it, that it would make me look weak or a risk in job interviews. I desperately wanted to talk to people again to whom I could admit to seeing a therapist or taking medication or having panic attacks or depression and not to feel like I had to be coated in bubble wrap or be told 'there, there'. I wanted a conversation about daily life where I didn't have to edit out my less palatable bits. That was the community I most missed. I found it again in Mental Health Mates, and have been going ever since.

Imogen's Black Dog: I think my animal would be a black snake. I know snakes have historically had a bad rap and I'm not helping the stereotype, but it's so tempting and easy to believe it when it lies to me. 'You've been rejected from a job; no one thinks you're worth paying a salary to; no one thinks you're worth keeping alive, you'd be better off dead' was a classic from that period last year. It digs out and contrives to find the worst-case intention behind the way everyone and everything reacts to me and it convinces me it's the only logical truth. It catastrophises and tells me it's just doing it to be kind, to protect me from the crushing feeling of getting my hopes up and then having them dashed again.

Maxine

I've been anxious and depressed throughout my life because I'm dyspraxic, which wasn't diagnosed until university. After a breakdown at nineteen, blogging – which was still new at the time – gave me the confidence to open up to others, online and in real life. I was always ambitious and determined not to let my problems stop me achieving what I wanted. But my life never progressed, always seeming like one step forward and two back.

By the age of thirty I had lost my job, lost two friends to suicide in three years and lost my business. After the second friend killed himself I became very ill and knew I needed to save myself from doing the same. In desperation, I came to the first MHM. The combination of mental ill-health and grief had left me feeling withdrawn and isolated, convinced everyone thought I was crazy and nobody understood. Even mutual friends who were grieving seemed to be avoiding me because they didn't want reminding of what had happened. A safe place to meet new like-minded people in person made such a difference to me at a very dark time.

Maxine's Black Dog: An inquisitive cat that runs into a corner sad-faced and scared when it gets too noisy.

Miranda

I think I was the very first person to respond to Bryony's tweet about the idea of a 'mental health mates group'. I was desperate to find a like-minded group of people who would understand my anxiety, low moments and wobbles. My friends are great but it's difficult to empathise when you really don't know what debilitating anxiety and depression feels like. One friend said, 'Just try and relax' – and that's my problem – I really can't and don't know how. It's isolating, lonely . . . I would give anything to not have the critical thoughts.

The very first MHM meeting was incredible. I came away feeling as high as a kite – like I had found a group that would be really supportive, non-judgemental and they knew what life in my head was like because they went through it too. They just 'got it' and made me feel less alone. Mental Health Mates is not a magic cure but it *is* the most incredible support network. We walk, talk, have picnics, go to the cinema and theatre – I think our second ever meeting was in a pub! – and the talking is not just about our struggles and worries – it's anything and everything. I never felt under pressure to share either – I could just be myself.

Miranda's Black Dog: It's a sly and nasty hyena because it laughs at you and always tells you how stupid you are – it's mean and nasty.

Polly

By the time Mental Health Mates had its first walk (February 2016), I'd been unable to work, aside from odd bits and pieces of writing and volunteering recommended by my therapist, for nearly two years. I'd lived with constant depression for nine years – mostly on a high-functioning level, having got through uni, worked full-time, and so on, whilst having talking therapies – and been on a wide range of largely ineffective anti-depressants. You name it, I'd tried it, right down to Buddhist meditation.

Having been through nervous breakdowns in 2011 and 2014, and several suicide attempts, I was feeling physically and emotionally isolated from the few friends I had left and, because so many people had drifted away or stopped relying on me for their needs, I really thought I was the problem.

At my lowest, I wondered if my depression had conjured up false memories of the friendships I remembered, or that they were some kind of psychotic episode sign, and that maybe I'd been alone all along. By February 2016, I finally had a really good psychologist, a psychiatrist, and I'd always had family support, but none of those can replace having your own friends, and this made it hard to progress very far with my recovery.

I remember feeling straight away that the people in Mental Health Mates supported each other. There was this immediate understanding that we were all in the same boat, and everyone's experience was valid. It was also a relief to talk about normal everyday things with people my own age; things like *Take Me Out*, or which films we wanted to see.

Polly's Black Dog: My depression would be a slug: it's hard to get rid of, not nice to look at, has a slimy but potent hold over me, and leaves a trail of destruction in its wake.

The connection I felt that morning with the people there was unlike anything I had experienced before. I even felt a bond with Chloe that had been hitherto absent. There was something special going on – it had that numinous thing my grandfather had attempted to tell me about all those years ago. Little did I know that some of the people who had showed up would go on to become my closest friends and allies, friends and allies who worked round the clock to make sure that Mental Health Mates became a proper thing, rather than a one-off stroll round a pond suggested by a mad woman. Little did I know that the numinous thing my grandfather spoke of was something I was about to start experiencing again and again and again. 'You're a long way from Alton Towers now,' said the girl, when I mentioned the walk at work the next day. At first I didn't know what she was talking about. Then she smiled, gave me a warm hug, and went to the canteen. 'Can I come to the next one?' she asked when she came back, handing me a congratulatory bag of Quavers, her eyes glistening with tears. 'I could do with it right now.' I was learning that though we may all look different on the outside, on the inside, we often have more in common than we realise.

2

To the Olympic Park

I should tell you now that I have never done anything by halves, be it pints of lager, tubs of ice cream, or major life decisions. And like almost everything else I have done during my time on the planet – getting a nice boyfriend, having a baby, paying bills – I completed *Mad Girl* by the skin of my teeth, a week after that first Mental Health Mates walk, three months before it was due to be published in hardback. I haven't mentioned that we were also in the process of selling our flat, because frankly, talking about selling your flat is really boring. Nobody buys a book and thinks, 'Gosh, I hope the author has dedicated several thousand words to the complicated rigmarole that is getting a mortgage; I hope there is a chapter about stamp duty and the mysterious ways in which solicitors move. By jove, it would be great if she penned an analysis of the nightmare that is putting an offer in on a house that is falling down, and what happened when the survey came back saying the building was unsafe to live in! What a quandary: live in unsafe house within catchment of outstanding primary school (perhaps rabbit hutch actually *in* the outstanding primary school?) or safe building next to an educational establishment that Ofsted has rated inadequate? I would simply LOVE TO READ THAT.'

Suffice it to say, attempting to finish a book, set up a network of mental health walks and buy a house was not a relaxing experience. But that was cool with me. I didn't want to be relaxed – if I did that, I might have to think about all the demons in my head, and that didn't really appeal to me at all. Indeed, Not Being Relaxed was a state I desired, on account of the fact I never had to pause or take stock. If I ever had a massage, I would talk nonstop during the treatment, until the therapist was forced to turn the whale music up so loudly that passersby might have thought they had accidentally stumbled across a secret Seaworld hidden inside a spa. When we went on holiday, I would make it my mission to make things as unrelaxing as possible. At airports and on planes I would hyperventilate, convinced that we were all about to die rather than go on a package holiday to Lanzarote. Once we went to Greece and I realised, upon arrival, that I had forgotten to pack my antidepressants. We then had to spend the first two days traipsing around the island, trying to find a morally corrupt pharmacist who spoke English and was willing to give me a packet of Prozac without a prescription. 'Why did you forget them?' pleaded my husband, whose plans to lie on the beach while Edie enjoyed the kids club had been scuppered by my inability to pack properly. 'You know you go funny without them.' 'It's not as if I did it on PURPOSE!' I sulked, once we had found a man who was willing to give me some drugs in return for 160 euros. But probably deep down in my subconscious I had done it on purpose, to avoid having to spend any time on a sunlounger with Jareth and the latest cool crime thriller. I mean, I love a crime thriller. But even they couldn't drown out the endless provocations from my friend the Goblin King, who was loudly telling me that back home in London, our flat had burned to the ground because I'd left a candle on or the ceiling had fallen through because I'd left a tap running.

If I just kept going at 150mph, even on holiday, then everything would be OK, surely?

People started to say to me: 'Crikey, Bryony, are you trying to be superwoman or something?' I took this as a compliment, even though it wasn't actually anywhere near the truth. In reality all I was trying to be was busy, so I could avoid being myself. Man, being myself sucked. I was seriously overweight which was fine until

Eat, Drink, Run.

I had to run for a bus. And even though I was almost in my mid-thirties and married with a child, life didn't look anything like I had imagined almost being in my mid-thirties and married with a child would. I was still drinking and smoking too much – I was just drinking and smoking too much once I had got my daughter down to bed. I was still feeling hungover every morning – I was just feeling hungover while attempting to wrestle a toddler into her clothes and feed her Weetabix. Sometimes, when I tried to give her a kiss before brushing my teeth in the morning, she would say, 'Mummy, you smell,' and Jareth told me that she was basically being parented by Shane McGowan, without the record deal or the talent or quite as good a set of teeth (just joking on the last count).

I had my second book coming out, sure, but I still had the same crippling self-esteem issues I had had when I was in my early twenties, crippling self-esteem issues that told me the book was a pile of crap that would perhaps scrape a C minus, if indeed it got graded at all. Jareth sat there, legs spread, and said, 'This is the work of a twelve-year-old. You should be thoroughly ashamed.' The thought of it coming out and being critically panned – or worse, completely ignored – filled me with such horror that I decided to throw myself wholesale into the process of moving. It was better, I felt, to spend my time obsessing over whether or not my inability to pay a council tax bill in my late

twenties was going to effect my ability to get a mortgage now. Replace one worry with another: that's the
way I like to do things.

And so when the email arrived inviting me to meet
the Duke and Duchess of Cambridge and Prince Harry,
I missed it. I missed a lot of emails – mostly people
only ever got in touch with me to tell me they hated
my columns or to sell me impotence drugs. My inbox
was like the digital equivalent of a skip – full of old
rubbish that only a tramp would ever be bothered to
sift through. I tried to tell myself that it was a mess
because I was simply too busy, too important. In reality
I was just too disorganised. The only lists I ever made
were To Don't Lists: don't check your inbox; don't
open letters that arrive in brown envelopes or written
in green ink; don't make lists. My motto was: 'if it's
important, they will call me', though of course this
assumed that 'they', whoever they were, had my tele-
phone number. And anyway, it wasn't as if I was
expecting an invite to hang with the royals. It wasn't
as if I woke up every day thinking, 'Hmm, I wonder
if today's the day that Wills and Kate will ask me
round for tea!' The thought of hanging out with the
future King of Great Britain was not one that crossed
my mind terribly often – in fact, it point blank hadn't.
I had never even entertained the idea. It was like
imagining that Brad Pitt might ask me on a date, or
that I might be asked by Victoria's Secret to 'walk'

the runway in their annual lingerie wankfest. It was, frankly, absurd.

I suppose I will have to call it fate, or that numinous thing again, that I just happened to be staring at my inbox that morning, refreshing it every thirty seconds in the hope that the 'reset password' link would appear from ASOS so I could go and buy a new bumper pack of leggings (as a sixteen-stone woman, leggings were really the only thing that felt comfortable any more, but I was always having to buy new pairs because my massive thighs meant that the seams would give way after about a week). 'FWD: INVITE: HRH Heads Together campaign launch next Monday' screamed the subject line. FWD, I thought – it must be important, or the sender must at the very least think it's important if they've resorted to sending it again. Also, I noticed the initials HRH. HRH was not, as far as I knew, some acronym for something internet related – in fact, from my lengthy time working for the *Daily Telegraph*, apparently Her Majesty's paper of choice, I recalled that HRH stood for something vaguely important, like Her Royal Highness or His Royal Highness or Hi why aren't you Replying to me Hi. I decided to open the email, if only so I could be sure I had been right to ignore it in the first place, and get on with buying my leggings.

'Hi Bryony,' it began. 'Just checking if you're able to make Monday? Thanks, Ben.' Who was Ben? What was happening on Monday? I scrolled down. Ben, it turned out, was a man who had been tasked with doing all the public relations for a mental health campaign called Heads Together, which was to be launched next week at the Olympic Park. The email that Ben had previously sent me not once, not twice, but *thrice*, explained that Heads Together was the brainchild of the Duke and Duchess of Cambridge and Prince Harry. 'We would like to invite you, as a journalist with a special interest in the subject, to attend the launch next Monday as a guest. This will be outside the traditional "royal rota" and will enable you to meet the charities and take part in the innovative activities that they are arranging to showcase their services to Their Royal Highnesses. While there won't be formal interview opportunities, it is our intention that you will have the opportunity to talk to Their Royal Highnesses while they take part in the event and be at the launch while they give their speeches to launch the campaign. I hope you can make it.'

I read this email about five times trying to make sense of it. During my career as a journalist I had had to cover royal events, which usually involved being kept 100 metres away from any actual royals, behind a barrier and several armed police. I would then be expected to bash out 1,000 words of colour about how beautiful the Duchess of Cambridge looked, even though I could only see her legs and would have had a better view staying at home and watching it on the telly.

I remember having to 'cover' the Royal Wedding. This involved getting up at 5 a.m., traipsing down to the Mall and squashing myself in with thousands of royalists to get a real sense of what was going on. 'We want you to write about the first kiss when they come out onto the balcony after they are married,' my editor explained. I was wedged into the armpit of a man who had been camping outside Buckingham Palace all week when the kiss actually happened – the only view I got was of the ground below me as I desperately tried not to gag from the stench of his body odour.

Then there was the time I had to go and stand outside the Lindo Wing of St Mary's Hospital all day to write a piece about the public's first glimpse of Prince George. I had only given birth myself less than three months before, and had been pulled out of maternity leave by my editor who thought it would be great to get the perspective of another new first-time mum, as if my experience of leaving hospital with a newborn was going to be in any way comparable to that of the Duchess of Cambridge. I wondered if she, too, had screamed at her husband for having the gall to immediately turn on Radio 4 the moment she had managed to strap the new baby into the car seat when he knew full well that she liked Radio 2. It seemed to me highly unlikely, though I suppose not entirely impossible. Childbirth does funny things to a woman, however regal they might happen to be.

It was one of the hottest days of the year and I had to scramble emergency childcare in the form of my sister. I thought, 'I will be there two hours, three max. She can do that. My daughter will barely notice I've gone.' When I arrived at the hospital I bumped into another journalist who kindly told me where all our colleagues were camping out. They were being made to sit in the gutter. Literally. They were in front of the photographers who were poised to catch every angle of the new addition, not to mention every detail of whatever outfit the poor Duchess of Cambridge had selected to wear when she emerged (I wondered if, like me, she would go for pyjamas and UGG boots). The other journalist told me that originally they had been standing in the gutter, but the snappers had furiously told them all to 'sit the fuck down' so that none of them would end up in the photos.

I did as they had been told, and sat in the gutter, careful to avoid fag ends and Coke cans discarded by the photographers, a row of bored-looking policemen standing in front of us staring back, as if to say, 'Are your parents proud of you?' This was what my so-called 'trade' had reduced me to, I thought. I am literally lying in the gutter, looking up at the stars. I sat there for four hours. Eventually, the summer heat broke and a giant thunderstorm started up. None of us moved in case the royals took it as an excuse to leg it while everyone was hiding inside the Costa Coffee across the road. Soaked and pining for my own baby, who was not going to rule the Commonwealth but was no less important for that, I attempted to gulp back tears. My phone was about to die when my sister called in a panic, telling me that Edie had filled four nappies in the last half an hour and I needed to come home IMMEDIATELY because it was gross and also she had a party to go to.

'You said two hours max!' she complained.

'I said three!'

'It's been almost five! What the hell are they doing in there? Why can't they just leave hospital like *normal* people?'

'Because they're not?'

'OK, good point. But look, I've got this work do to go to and I am NOT turning up with my twelve-week-old niece, especially not now she's decided to poo for Britain. I mean, how could so much *stuff* come out of something so small!'

To be honest, I was relieved that my daughter had decided to take this opportunity to gross out my sister. I was no more capable of being a royal reporter right now than I was a midwife. I called my editor and told her my baby was ill – furthermore, it didn't look like anyone was leaving the hospital within the next month or so. Clearly feeling bad because legally she wasn't actually allowed to ask me to work during my maternity leave, and had just been chancing it, she told me it would be OK to go home. I walked round the corner to the tube, and as I got there I heard a huge cheer go up that suggested the new family had left hospital. Oh well, I thought, I'll get a better look of the baby on Twitter than I would have done from that filthy gutter anyway.

So, my experiences of covering royal events had left me somewhat of a republican. It wasn't the fault of the royals – it was just that if they were all to suddenly decide that they couldn't be arsed with the faff of being held accountable for every cough, spit and fart of their existence, my job would almost certainly involve less feeling like a leper, and less scrambling around in crowds concerned that I was about to develop severe agoraphobia. No wonder I had taken to writing about my depression – anything was preferable to sitting in gutters with fag ends.

But here I was being invited not as an annoying hack, but as a proper person – or at the very least, an annoying hack who happened to have an interest in mental health. If this email was real, and not some terrible prank, then I would not have to stand behind railings in the hope of glimpsing the Duchess of Cambridge's hair. I would actually be able to see it for myself! Maybe even *touch* it, though obviously in a way that looked entirely accidental so as to avoid arrest.

I was going to have to work out how to do that, but I had time—

Hang on, I didn't. Not really. It was Friday. The launch was on Monday. How rude of me! To be fair, though, I would have expected an invitation from the palace to arrive by horse-drawn carriage, or fairy godmother, not email. Was this how modern royals did things now? I quickly typed out my reply to this 'Ben' character. 'I apologise for the lateness of my reply – I have been ill,' I lied. 'However your invite has made me feel much, much better, and I would love to come!' I pressed send. I briefly wondered if 'Ben' was now sitting at his desk cursing himself for having sent the email to the wrong Bryony. 'No, no, not the mad, disorganised Bryony who happens to be a journalist with a special interest in mental health! The OTHER ONE!' But if that had happened, Ben was too polite to mention it. 'Great, thank you for getting back to me,' he responded. 'Look forward to meeting you on Monday. Best wishes, Ben.'

I couldn't wait to meet Ben. And Hazza. And Wills and Kate. Could I call them that? Probably not. And what was I going to wear? Not leggings, that's for sure. Even if I wanted to, they weren't going to show up on time given that ASOS *still* hadn't sent me through a new password.

That day, I receive two pieces of good news: we have got a mortgage and are moving into our falling-down house, and a girl in Leeds would like to start up a Mental Health Mates there. I don't know which is more pleasing – they are both as wonderful as each other, really.

By this point we have had three Mental Health Mates walks in London, each one bigger than the last. On these walks, people are talking to each other about the efficacy of certain antidepressants with the ease that you would normally discuss football down the pub. They are discussing therapies they have tried, episodes they have had. We now have a Whatsapp group for all the people who are keen to help build this into a proper thing – a Whatsapp group being the modern-day way of making something official, don't you think? That there are people who want to be part of this blows me away given that a couple of months ago I was finding it hard to leave the flat. There is even a group who have started going to a weekly pub quiz together. I feel all warm and cosy inside, as I imagine the Waltons did every time they went to bed. Is this how normal people feel on a daily basis? Is this the hallowed sense of happiness that everybody is constantly searching for? Am I actually achieving something worthwhile? Could it be that things are going to actually turn out OK?

I wake up the next day and the Black Elephant is there. He's sitting at the end of the bed, vying for space with

Eat, Drink, Run.

Jareth the Goblin King. I look for my husband but he is nowhere to be seen; we went out last night to celebrate the news that we would be able to move to the new house and get our daughter into the really good primary school, and I think he must have fallen asleep on the sofa downstairs. My head hurts – I must have drunk at least five pints of strong continental lager plus two glasses of cheap champagne – but the thing I notice most is the feeling of doom in my gut. I would do anything just to have a headache, a mundane, purely physical sense of pain in my body. Right now, I realise the other pain is back, the emotional pain, the one that tells me the world is about to end.

I should have known this would happen. The moment I think that things might actually be all right, that I might even be close to contentment, another part of my brain tells me not to be so bloody sure. As a child, my mum used to say that I would worry when I had nothing to worry about. But now I wonder that after a lifetime of anxiety, it's almost as if I don't believe I deserve to feel good – as if I have to punish myself every time some part of my brain dares to send messages of positivity out to the rest of my body. How to describe this feeling without making you all feel bleak? I can't. It feels like the apocalypse is coming. All the crazy things I did when I was high on coke in my twenties – the casual sex, the throwing up, the falling over – are going to come back to haunt me, and the Mental Health Mates are going to realise I am evil, not mentally ill, and dump me. Ben – and please remember that I have still not met Ben, that I have no idea if Ben is even someone I would want to be friends with – is going to find out that I am bad for the royal reputation and rescind the invitation. The security detail will arrest me on the door. I'm going down. It is only a matter of time.

I try to clear my head in a variety of ways, none of which seem to work: I make porridge for my daughter, put a wash on, unload the dishwasher, have a shower. Under the hot water the panic seems to bloom, rising from my gut up to my oesophagus and then out of my mouth. I brush my teeth and in the steamy bathroom I start to cry. It is all useless. All of it. No matter what I do, no matter how hard I try, I always end up back here, in a pit of anxiety entirely of my own making. If I hadn't gone and got drunk last night, things might be better. If I hadn't gone and got drunk and high the whole way through my twenties, things would be better. If I wasn't such a fat, unhealthy mess, things would be better. If this, if that . . . the only thing that seems certain is that the whole world is going to fall down on my head.

My husband finds me in the bathroom and starts to talk very slowly to me. 'What. We. Are. Going. To. Do. Is. Get. Dressed. And. Go. Out. To. The. Park. Where. We. Will. Go. To. The. Swings. And. Then. Get. Some.

Eat, Drink, Run.

Lunch. We. Will. Go. For. A. Walk. Then. We. Are. Going. To. Come. Back. Here. And. I. Am. Going. To. Play. Dollies. With. Edie. And. You. Are. Going. To. Do. Absolutely. Nothing. Because. You. Are. Doing. Too. Much. And. I. Am Worried. You. Are. About. To. Have. A. Breakdown.'

'I will definitely have a breakdown if I do absolutely nothing,' I reply, very quickly, at least treble the speed of him. 'If I do absolutely nothing everything is going to overwhelm me. I don't want to do absolutely nothing. Doing absolutely nothing is my idea of hell; it's how you would feel if I told you that we were going to sit down and talk about our emotions for two hours. Do not make me do absolutely nothing. And if you are going to absolutely insist on me doing absolutely nothing, then I am going to need to tuck into my stash of valium.'

Harry shakes his head, then hugs me.

The rest of the weekend is a fuggy blur.

The Olympic Park is not that far on the tube. My phone says it should take approximately fifty-three minutes door to door. Simple. And yet just getting out of bed that Monday morning feels like it requires heavy lifting. Getting up and out and making my way to the station feels like I am wading through treacle. I feel as if I deserve . . . well, an Olympic medal. I haven't eaten properly since that porridge on Saturday morning, just

70

slept in a haze of depression and diazepam. My stomach keeps making strange noises. My throat keeps trying to burp. What if when I meet the royals I involuntarily let out a giant belch? That's probably going to happen, isn't it? The room is going to fall silent just as I do it, and I will end up on the *Mail*'s Sidebar of Shame: 'JUST WHO DOES SHE THINK SHE IS? LARGER LADY IN LEGGINGS LETS RIP AT THE ROYALS!'

It's a really beautiful May day. The sun is shining. By rights I should be over the moon; but I don't do rights, just wrongs. I am sweating in my dress (I haven't actually worn leggings, don't worry). I keep checking in a compact that my make-up hasn't melted off my face. I am exhausted from all the diazepam I have taken, and wondering if prescribed drugs are really any better than the ones that I used to buy from a dodgy dealer.

By the time the Central line pulls into Stratford, I am a gibbering wreck. I realise I would rather be behind the barriers or in the gutter than actually attending something as a person in my own right. At least there I would be with the other journalists. At least there I *belong*. But I don't know anyone who is going to be at this reception at the Olympic Park – not even Ben. Who will I talk to? Will I be shunned? Will Ben finally announce that it has all been a terrible mistake and that I need to leave? I realise, as I walk up to the policeman standing next to the security barriers at the entrance of the park, that I have bought the Black Elephant and Jareth the Goblin King with me. But I remember that they were never invited in the first place, and that even if they were, they probably haven't brought their ID with them. 'Sorry guys,' I say to them. 'You're not allowed in here. You're going to have to turn back and go home.' And then I take a deep breath and step towards the policeman.

I may be a 35-year-old woman with a career and family, but in my head I am seven-year-old Bryony, about to walk into a children's party where I don't know any of the guests. With my leotard stuck up my bum. That happened once. It was a ballet-themed do for the goddaughter my mother never saw – I was her guilt offering, her sacrificial lamb to atone for years of neglect. 'I know I haven't bothered to send you a card since you were one, that I have ignored all your mother's phone calls for the past five years because of what happened at that party when we had drunk a bit too much *vino tinto*, but that's all in the past now. Here is my daughter, dressed as a beautiful ballerina, in so much as one can be a beautiful ballerina when her leotard is stuck up her bum. Never mind, pretend you didn't see it. Right, is it OK if I leave her here while I go and get my hair done? It is a drop-off party, yes? Be right back!'

The memory still haunts me to this day.

The policeman checks my ID against a list of names and lets me through. Could this be for *real?* The launch is at a restaurant near the foot of the Orbit, a 114-metre-high tower that looks almost exactly how my brain currently feels – confused, on high alert, a little bit all over the place. I keep trying to remember what I have been told by the one colleague I know who has actually met royalty – do not call the Duchess of Cambridge 'Kate'. She is m'am as in jam, and if you really do find yourself having to call her by a first name, then you better make sure it is Catherine. 'Only the tabloids call her Kate,' my friend warns. 'It's really not very classy.' Also: do not overexaggerate the curtsey lest you fall over/end up looking like a prat. 'Less is more,' continued my friend, thus neatly flipping on its head the maxim by which I have always lived my life.

I pass the reporters outside and give them my best royal wave as a bit of a laugh. I'm not sure how well that goes down, but as it's likely to be the only time I ever get to do it, I decide I am going to make the most of being in this exalted position, nowhere near any gutters. Inside the restaurant is a hive of activity. The Heads Together campaign will be raising money and awareness for eight mental health charities: Mind, which works nationally to provide services for the mentally ill; Best Beginnings, which helps parents; Calm, which helps men; The Mix and Young Minds; which both support young adults; The Anna Freud

Centre, which helps children; Contact, which works with servicemen and women; and finally, Place 2 Be. I find myself next to the latter's stand, learning about the work they do going into schools and educating children about mental health. Three primary school kids have come along to explain how Place 2 Be has helped them; they talk about mental health in the same way they would physical health, as if they were discussing how embarrassing it is to get nits or the pain of having your BCG.

The three royals then take to a small stage and explain that they decided to set up Heads Together because they felt that the common thread between all the charity work they did, be it helping children, the homeless, or the armed forces, was mental health. Heads Together, they add, will be the official charity of the 2017 London Marathon. And I stand there at the back of the room gulping back tears, over-whelmed with emotion for twelve-year-old me, pondering how different things might have been had Place 2 Be existed back when I was a kid, how different things might have been for so many of us had royals previously used their platform to talk about mental health.

But I also feel joy – pure, unadulterated joy. The Olympic Park is a place where many seemingly insur-mountable challenges have been conquered – now it feels as if we are finally on the way to conquering the most insurmountable of all: breaking the stigma surrounding mental health. It takes my breath away. The sense of hope and optimism I feel in that moment is the only way I can explain what I do next.

Finally, I meet Ben. Honestly, the amount of thinking I've done about his email over the last weekend, it's almost as exciting as the prospect of meeting Kate Middleton. Sorry, I mean the Duchess of Cambridge. In my fevered state I have imagined that Ben is six foot something, suited and booted, perhaps the kind of guy who would give David Gandy a run for his money – surely everyone who works for the young royals is gorgeous and ripped and able to take out a lunatic with one flick of their little finger. Actually, as it turns out, Ben is quite short and has no hair. If I wanted to make a run for Prince Harry and handcuff myself to his ankles, I am pretty sure Ben would struggle to stop me, all sixteen stone something of me. I could squash Ben with ease. I could eat him, probably. But I don't want to find myself on the wrong side of him because he is my ticket to a better life. Or at least a life where I can go to the pub and tell people that I once shook hands with Kate Middleton. Sorry, the Duchess of Cambridge.

Ben, it turns out, is not a member of their security detail but in charge of the PR for Heads Together. He is polite but I am sure that under that diplomatic veneer he can't believe he is having to deal with a buffoon like me. He tells me he is going to introduce me to the 'principals'.

'The who?' I say, confused.

'The principals,' he responds. 'The Duke and Duchess of Cambridge and Prince Harry.'

I want to reply: 'How exciting! I now know the secret code word for Kate Middleton and her husband and brother-in-law! This is beyond any of my wildest dreams! I thought I would be able to wow people with reports on Kate's hair, but now I can also sound extremely knowledgeable by referring to them as "the principals"! People in the pub will think I'm the complete bee's knees!' But instead I say: 'Oh, of course. I've been practising my curtseys all weekend in preparation.'

Ben looks alarmed. 'You don't have to curtsey,' he says. 'In fact, we'd prefer it if you didn't. The whole point of this campaign is that everyone feels comfortable talking about their mental health. It's letting people know that deep down, we are all the same.' Secretly, I am relieved. But before I have any time to continue our conversation, an extremely well-spoken man is barrelling up to me and . . . oh my, he's introducing me to Prince William.

Very suddenly, every camera in the room is trained on us. My heart rate starts to soar. Sweat begins to pool above my top lip. 'Hello Bryony,' says the future king of Great Britain. 'I have read your pieces on mental health and just wanted to thank you for writing them. We need more people like you out there spreading the word.'

Aware that we are surrounded by photographers, I do not pull the face I instinctively want to pull – one that involves shaking my head and screwing up my cheeks in disbelief, as if to say, 'You? YOU HAVE READ MY ARTICLES? GIVE OVER!' I can hear Jareth calling from outside, where he is stuck behind the security barriers. 'AS IF HE'S EVER READ ANYTHING YOU'VE WRITTEN!' Jareth is shouting. 'HE'S JUST BEING POLITE. AND BY THE WAY YOU'RE SHAKING AND SWEATING AND LOOK LIKE A COMPLETE TIT!'

I breathe deeply and try to block Jareth out. 'Thank you, Sir,' I say, immediately worrying that Sir is not the correct greeting, and that I am about to be sent to the Tower. Prince William starts telling me about his work as an air ambulance pilot, and how a great many of the call-outs he goes on are to suicides or attempted suicides. I am so focused on not panicking that my face breaks into a huge smile, which is so *not* the reaction you are supposed to have when talking about suicide. I mutter, witter, and tell him that I will keep on writing about mental health until I am blue in the face. Which I might actually be, right now. He shakes my hand, and is gone.

Eat, Drink, Run.

'Well,' I hear Jareth call from outside. 'At least you never have to go through the embarrassment of seeing him again.'

By the time I am introduced to the Duchess of Cambridge, my nerves have calmed a little. I am totally in control of this, I think. In fact, our conversation is going to be so amazing that by the end of it she's going to ask for my number and we are going to become friends, and our children will go on play dates together and we will have spa days together, BFFs to the end.

What actually happens is this:

The Duchess of Cambridge: We really appreciate you being part of this.
Me [thinking what lovely hair she has]: It's my pleasure.
The Duchess of Cambridge: We've got to get as many voices out there as we can. We need to keep talking because the more that we do, the more people realise how important the issue is.
Me: You know that Heads Together is the official charity of the marathon next year?
The Duchess of Cambridge: Yes, isn't it brilliant?
Me: Yes, it is! I was wondering, are you going to run it?

The Duchess of Cambridge [laughing nervously]:
Well, I think there might be some security issues
with that.
Me [motioning to my fuller figure]: Well, if I can
do it, anyone can!
Ben: Did you just volunteer to run the marathon
for Heads Together?
Me: Um, did I?
Ben: You totally did.
The Duchess of Cambridge: Wonderful!

So that, I suppose, is that.

3

To the Pub

'You're doing what?'

Harry is sitting in the garden of our flat, a bottle of rosé in front of him and a look of horror on his face. I have just told him about my plan to run the London Marathon next year – I call it 'my' plan as if I have come up with it all by myself, like a responsible human who sets themselves goals, and neglect to give him the details of what really happened.

'I'm doing the London Marathon,' I repeat confidently, because if I say it enough times like I really mean it then I might actually start to believe it myself. 'I'm doing it to raise money for Heads Together. Heads Together is the mental health campaign set up by my friend Catherine.'

Harry begins to look even more confused.

Eat, Drink, Run.

'Catherine. As in the Duchess of Cambridge,' I explain, with a shake of my head.

'As in Kate Middleton?' he replies.

'You might want to call her that, but I wouldn't dream of it.'

'Right,' nods Harry, a hint of sarcasm evident in the shake of his head.

'Maybe I will do it dressed as Jareth the Goblin King,' I continue. 'Wouldn't that be a great, like, metaphor or something?'

'OK, now I think you've completely lost it,' Harry says, lighting a fag. (I should point out here that I am also smoking a cigarette and drinking a glass of wine.) 'I always knew you were mad but now I reckon you might actually be certifiable. You're telling me that you are going to do a *marathon*. And that not only are you going to do a marathon, but you're going to do it in tight silver trousers and a David Bowie wig.'

'Actually, I was thinking that as I already have the blonde hair I could probably just style it on the morning with a bit of gel, thus negating the need for a wig.'

'OK. Listen, Bryony. I don't often tell you not to do something. I realised, a long time ago, that you wouldn't listen to me anyway. Like all those times we've been on nights out and I say, "It's time to go home, darling" because it's 2 a.m., and you've replied with a "Fuck off, Harry, I'm having fun." I know that there is no saying no to you. But I'm thinking about your mental health here. I'm well aware that running is good for it – but there's a difference between going for a twenty-minute jog around the park and taking on a marathon. Do you know how long a marathon is?'

'Of course I do!' I am indignant.

'Then how long is it?'

'What is this? A test? I thought we were having a nice evening drinking rosé in the garden, not doing a quiz.'

'I think it's fairly important that when you decide you are going to do a marathon, you know how long it is.'

'OK. It's 26.4 miles.'

'Actually, it's 26.2.'

'Brilliant! Point two of a mile less than I thought it was. Easy!'

'Bryony, you do know that the first person to do a marathon *died*?'

I didn't. I stay quiet.

'Know your Greek history,' he continues, stubbing out his cigarette.

'I have to say that you're beginning to sound quite smug,' I respond, lighting another one. 'And smug is NOT a good look.'

'Neither is collapsing and dying while training for a marathon. So listen. It's around 490 BC. The Persians are all up in the Greeks' grill, trying to take their beautiful country, and there's this battle in this town called Maratho—'

Eat, Drink, Run.

'Get to the point please.'

'I am. So there's this battle in this town called Marathon, and the Greeks win, which marks a real turning point in the Greco–Persian wars.'

'Fascinating,' I say sourly.

'And there's this man called Pheidippides who fought in the battle, and he is dispatched to Athens to tell them that the Greeks have won. So he runs the whole way there, bursts into the Greek assembly and says, "We have won!" Then he collapses and dies. And do you know how long the distance was between Marathon and Athens?'

'Don't tell me: 26.4 miles.'

'No, Bryony. 26.2 miles! 26.2 miles!'

'Whatever. That was 490 BC. There has been a whole heap of scientific advances since then. Like bottled water. And Jelly Babies. Perhaps if Pheidiwhatever-hisname had had Jelly Babies, he would have been OK. Also, he had just fought in a battle. It's unlikely that on the morning of the London Marathon I will have fought in any battle other than the daily one we have to get Edie to eat some fruit with her porridge. And also, it was Greece. It's really hot in Greece. Not so much in London. Trying to compare what I am going to do with what this dude did several millennia ago is disingenuous to say the least.'

'OK,' says Harry, nodding. I am pouring more wine into my glass. 'But do you really need to take on a marathon? You've got a book that's about to come out. You've got Mental Health Mates. You've got a daily job as a columnist at a newspaper. You've got a house move coming up. And you've got me and Edie. Is adding marathon training into that really a great idea? Marathons are *hard*, you know. Really hard.'

I look at Harry in disbelief. Is this really the man I married? Does he have even the slightest awareness of who *he* has married? 'No shit, Sherlock,' I shoot back. 'Of course marathons are hard. That's why people do them. To challenge themselves, to prove a point, to let the world know that they are ALIVE and that they haven't dropped down dead like what's-his-gob. I am under absolutely no illusions about the task I have taken on. Yes, running a marathon is going to be hard. But do you know what, Harry?'

He shakes his head, wafts his fag, smoke billowing in the air.

'Moving for 26.2 miles can't be any harder than the days when I haven't been able to move at all because of the weight of mental illness on me. Believe me. There's no way it can be more difficult than *that*.'

Denial is a powerful emotion. It is not a river in Egypt, as my husband likes to say to me every time a book deadline is looming and I appear not to have written a single word. Its purpose is to put off something you do not want to do, to avoid a reality you are not particularly keen on engaging with. So while I know I am going to do the 26.2 miles, while I know that there is absolutely no way I'm not going to be part of the first mental health marathon, for the time being, while there is still almost a year to go before race day (shudder), I am going to ignore it. It is not my priority. It doesn't even feel like a reality, just a vaguely abstract thing some place in the very distant future that I have tentatively agreed to – the equivalent of agreeing to host Christmas for both your family and the in-laws next year, because next year is next year and anything could happen between now and then. Like serious illness, for example. Or nuclear war. Or Donald Trump becoming president of the United States.

Right now my priority is moving house. Plus there is the small matter of *Mad Girl* coming out. Publication day and moving day are ridiculously close to one another – in fact, they are just a few days apart. This means that once we have relocated, I will have exactly twenty-four hours to breathe deeply before embarking on the lunacy that is a book tour. Honestly, as if writing books about mental illness isn't enough to make you break down (which, let's face it, it is), then try grappling with the idea of promoting one. What if everybody hates it? Worse, what if everyone is completely indifferent to it? What if nobody actually reads it? All that pain, all that misery, all that time picking open an old scar and turning it into a festering, bloody, open wound? All of that will have been for absolutely nothing.

I tell this to my editor who says, very kindly, that people will read it – even if by people she means her and everyone else at the publishing house who has been forced to wade through the contents of my head. Jareth tells me it is puerile rubbish, that it would be deluded to think of it as anything else. I am spending entire hours self-flagellating. It is not good enough. I am not good enough. I will never be good enough. My career is about to end.

My OCD is creeping back in, the time it takes to leave the house gradually getting longer and longer – the oven is off, but why don't you just go back and check a few more times to be absolutely sure; and while you're there, how about you make sure all the candles aren't burning too? I realise one morning that in order to get out of the house I have to take pictures on my phone of the gas hobs and leave outside the front door all the lovely scented candles that have been given to me as gifts by unsuspecting normal people who have no idea about the torturous processes that go through my head every time I even try and venture to the corner shop. My brain says: it would be just like you to burn the flat down right now, just as we are about to move out, leaving us penniless and destitute and without a roof over our heads. I am so gripped with anxiety all the time that it doesn't even strike me as ridiculous that Jareth is now taking it upon himself to make me feel like an arsonist. I suppose, in the grand scheme of things, arson is kind of low down the list of worries that include being a serial killer and a paedophile; but then anxiety is anxiety and it's all pretty grim, however it might happen to manifest.

Harry suggests I go to see my psychiatrist, so I can tell her that I am feeling 'stressed'. It seems like as good an idea as any right now – I cannot let Jareth in and allow him to cause a full-on breakdown what with the house move and the book coming out. I don't have the *time* to be ill; becoming sick would be really inconvenient (I do not realise that even thinking this is a sign that I am most likely already really sick).

I get to her office on autopilot. 'How are you?' she asks, sitting serenely in her seat. 'I'm fine,' I lie. She continues to look at me serenely, in silence, in that way that only therapists can. Thirty seconds pass. I begin to feel uncomfortable. 'I'm fine,' I repeat. 'But how are you *really*?' she asks, tilting her head and looking at me with something that could be pity but surely isn't pity because she's a psychiatrist and isn't looking at someone in pity unprofessional?

It doesn't matter, in the end. Maybe I feel like being pitied. Maybe a little bit of pity is going to go a long way right now. Just to have someone ask me how I am *really*, just to have someone cut through the pasted-on cheery face and see past the Bryony bullshit . . .

well, that is enough. That is enough to turn me from vaguely functioning human into a snotty mess.

'I'm OK,' I sob. 'I'm OK.'

It is clear I am not.

'I'm just . . .'

A deep, guttural sound comes out of my mouth, the kind of sound that you might expect to hear from a wounded animal. The psychiatrist continues to make no noise at all.

'I'm, I'm, I'm . . .'

More guttural sounds. Why isn't she saying anything? Why can't she say something? Something like: 'I can tell from the way you are sobbing precisely what is wrong with you and now I have worked out precisely what is wrong with you I am going to write you a prescription for a form of medication that is going to make everything better. Thanks for coming, that will be £150!'

Instead: nothing. I am paying her to say absolutely nothing.

'I'm OK,' I repeat. 'I mean, I'm not OK.' Nice work, Bryony. Nice work. If you can't even lie to yourself, what hope have you of pulling it off with this psychiatrist? 'Oh God, I'm sorry.'

I wail.

'Why are you sorry?'

Finally, she speaks!

'For coming here and crying on you.'

Eat, Drink, Run.

'Believe me, you're not the first,' she says, motioning to the box of tissues that sits on the table between us. 'That's what people tend to come to me to do. It's kind of my job. Now why don't you tell me what's going on?'

So I do. I tell her about the house and the book and Mental Health Mates and how I suspect I might be drinking too much and that the drinking too much is possibly making things seem worse. 'I mean, alcohol is a depressant,' I announce to her proudly, as if knowing this fact makes me very wise. She nods. 'Cutting down on alcohol intake is a good idea if you are feeling stressed or depressed,' she says. 'That's not to say that you can't have the odd glass of red here or there. Everything in moderation. But while you are feeling vulnerable, it's good to cut it out.'

'Is there a medication I can take that will make me want to stop drinking? Like, something that will remove all the cravings?' I am only half joking when I say this.

The psychiatrist suddenly looks both serious and sad, neither of which were reactions I was going for. 'There is a medication that makes you very very ill if you drink alcohol, but I'm not going to give it to you. In some people, even the alcohol in their perfume causes an extreme reaction that can leave them hospitalised. But you know that if you're feeling that desperate to stop, and that unable to stop, then there are always AA meetings.'

90

Now it is my turn to be silent.

'In my experience they really are the best way to get sober.'

'You don't get it,' I say to her, almost in disbelief. 'I'm not an alcoholic. I may occasionally be a problem drinker, but I'm not an alcoholic. I have a job. I have a family and soon I will have a house. I have a book coming out. I've just signed up to do a marathon. Alcoholics don't do that. I'm just talking about *managing* my drinking for a bit. I can do that. I only came because I was feeling so overwhelmed and I thought you might be able to up my dose of antidepressants or something. We've been talking about it for a while, and maybe it's time.'

'Maybe it is,' she nods. 'But you know that upping antidepressants can make you feel very unstable for a couple of weeks. Are you sure that's something you want?'

'If in a few weeks I feel better than this, then yes.'

My psychiatrist nods. 'OK. We'll go up to 60mg. But just to be safe I am also going to prescribe you something called quetiapine, which is a form of anti-psychotic.'

'Anti-psychotic?'

'Yes. Don't be alarmed. It sounds scary but anti-psychotics are medicines that are fairly common to prescribe to people who tend to suffer from major depressive episodes.'

'Oh,' I say.

'It'll just take the edge off things while we get the dose right on your Prozac.'

'Uh-huh,' I nod.

She writes a prescription. 'Any questions?' she asks.

'No. I mean, well, yes. I just wondered, if, say, I had a work do to go to or a birthday or something or a book launch even and I got offered a glass of champagne, say, would it be OK to drink on this?'

'If you're just planning to stick to one glass of champagne, sure.' She looks me square in the eye. 'And remember what I said about AA. It's really not as frightening as you'd think. You might even find it helpful.'

Harry suggests that I should take a break before embarking on the move and the promotional tour. 'Why don't you go away for a night to a hotel spa with Chloe?'

My brain wants to respond: 'Why don't I take a break? Maybe because the flat needs to be packed into boxes and movers need to be booked and solicitors need to be pushed into getting the fuck on with things, none of which are things that you're going to do.' But he's right. The idea of a night away at a spa does sound appealing, if only because from now on I am going to be living if not in an actual cardboard box, then surrounded by them, unable to locate my toothbrush or knickers or moustache removal cream. Yeech. A week without that and I end up looking like Poirot. I FaceTime Chloe, who is not exactly keen on the idea. 'Every time I've gone away with you for a "nice, relaxing break" I have ended up feeling like I need another nice, relaxing break, only this time, an ACTUAL nice, relaxing break as opposed to the shit show of madness that happens to take place with a nice, relaxing landscape in the background. Do you remember when we went to Croatia? You became mates with the mad gay couple in the room next door and ended up disappearing for twenty-four hours while they fed you Ecstasy at a festival in some woods. I felt like your mother. Then there was the time that we went on that press trip to the Brecon Beacons that was billed as a "walking weekend" except that the only walking we did was into doors because we spent the whole time in the hotel bar. Your idea of a nice, relaxing break is very different to most people's idea of a nice, relaxing break, in that it involves nothing nice or relaxing. So when you come to me and say you need to get away for a night before the book comes out, I've got to tell you that I am suspicious. I feel nervous. But I also see that you've had a hell of a lot on your plate over the last few months and so I am willing to suspend my disbelief for once and trust that maybe, just maybe, you really do want a nice, relaxing break.'

Eat, Drink, Run.

'I've agreed to do a marathon,' I suddenly blurt out.

'Oh God,' Chloe says, plunging her head into her hands. 'I take it all back.'

I book a night at a hotel in the Cotswolds that I have seen on Instagram via the feeds of various cool people I follow but have never actually met. I don't buy that Instagram makes you feel bad – when I am feeling particularly low I click on hashtags like #maldives and #sohofarmhouse and imagine myself sitting outside in a tin bath with a glass of champagne in my hand, Nick Grimshaw and Alexa Chung laughing gaily around me, and for a short while everything feels OK again. But there's only so far that the *idea* of going away for a bit can take you, and at some point you actually have to attempt to do it for real. Surely I can do 'nice and relaxing', just for one night? Will twenty-four hours in a five-star country house hotel kill me? It's unlikely. What's the worst that can happen? I spend the whole time in the jacuzzi stressing about the move and the book? Someone massages me with neroli oil rather than lavender? I go for a walk and step in a cow pat? It's going to be *fine*, I tell myself.

And what happens next is proof of why I try not to do that too often.

As nice and relaxing breaks go, it couldn't have got off to a nicer or more relaxing start. Chloe drives us, because I don't have a licence. It's not that I've lost it – I've just failed to get one. I've never even had a lesson. I had always put this down to the fact that I grew up in London, where the public transport was so good that I never needed to get a driving licence. Again, this may be denial at play. In reality it probably had more to do with the fact that I was having too good a time going out and drinking to ever bother with attempting to do something that might interfere with that. But anyway, even if I could drive, I wouldn't be safe behind the wheel right now. The quetiapine I am taking seems to be blurring the edges of everything, so the world is in a sort of soft focus. With one pop of a pill, Jareth can go from sitting on my lap illegally in the front of the car to being locked in the boot. I am completely oblivious to his muffled screams or his thumping on the roof. This, I believe, is what some people refer to as 'being high'.

'I find it incredible,' says Chloe, as we pootle down the M4 in her Mini, 'that you have got to the grand old age of thirty-five without ever having driven anything more than a bumper car.'

I look up from my phone. 'Actually, I've never even done that.'

'You're kidding me?' says Chloe, glancing across in disbelief.

'Keep your eyes on the road,' I snap.

'So you're telling me that the only thing you've ever

driven is your husband, mad? Sometimes, it amazes me that you have actually managed to keep yourself alive for this long.'

'Me too, Chloe. Me too.'

'And if you can't even manage to get driving lessons, I am seriously worried about your ability to train for a marathon. It's a big ask, Bryony. A REALLY big ask.'

'Chloe, the whole point of a marathon is that it involves using your feet. Surely, given the fact I have always relied on them rather than a car, that is a sign that I will be fine with a marathon. I'm an expert at using my feet!' I wiggle my toes for effect, then realise that she can't see this as they are hidden in the foot-well. 'While you are all stuck in traffic jams listening to Capital FM, I'm out there putting one foot in front of the other. It's going to be a doddle.'

'You get Ubers everywhere,' retorts Chloe, before turning the radio up loud.

The hotel is beautiful, set in acres of luscious grounds. It is late May and the sun is out, that glorious spring weather that instils you with hope after a long winter in the dark. It's like waking up from a long sleep to find that the sun is streaming through the window and your other half has made you breakfast in bed – bliss. Or maybe it's just the effect of the quetiapine. Whatever it is, it's working. I float around the property like a woodland nymph, albeit one who takes a size eighteen to twenty dress. We go swimming in the outdoor pool, and have massages in the spa. We have even had a room upgrade, and been put in a spacious suite set over several floors with two bedrooms. In the late afternoon I lie back on the bed and doze off to sleep. For a moment, just a moment, I feel invincible.

After our naps, we head for some food at the hotel restaurant, sitting outside on the terrace in the evening sun. Birds sing in the trees. It is warm enough that we don't need our jackets. Even Chloe looks – well, nice and relaxed. 'Gordon,' she says, perusing the menu, 'I think you might just have pulled this off for once.'

'Shall we have some champagne to celebrate?' I suggest.

'Why not?'

So we order a bottle.

When I come round I am in bed fully clothed and all the lights are on. I squint at the alarm clock on the table and see that it is just after 3 a.m. I realise that my contacts are still in. Then I am hit by the overpowering stench of . . . vomit. I look down and see that I am covered in it. Underneath me is a towel – there are also towels on the floor beneath the bed. I dread to think what is under them. I dread to think but it doesn't matter, because I already know. More vomit. I try to get up but realise that I can't. My left leg is throbbing in pain. Instead, I sit up. The towel moves under my weight to reveal dinner from the night before: a spring vegetable risotto now regurgitated and sautéed in bile. I pull off my dress and survey the damage. Just below my left knee is a bruise and under that bruise, I feel, is a hard lump. My right calf is covered in cuts and I see that there is also blood on the towel below me. The nausea and the physical wounds fade into the background as my familiar friend anxiety blooms in my stomach.

Finally, I manage to get up. I haul myself to the bathroom to go for a pee. When I look in the mirror some sort of deranged harpy appears to be staring back – hair on end, covered in sick, mascara all over her face. Her eyes are bloodshot, the whites tinged ever-so-slightly yellow. The deranged harpy splashes water over her face. The deranged harpy is me.

I try to brush my teeth and take my make-up off. When I go back into the bedroom I am appalled at the full horror of what confronts me: sick everywhere, barely touched bottles of water on the bedside table. Looking out of the window I see a dozen or so shot glasses on the garden furniture, and a teacup saucer full of fag ends. The teacup, I will later discover, is half full of beer. Things start to flash through my mind, torturous images of what I presume to have been the night before: falling down some stairs; a member of staff picking me up off the floor; being told off by the couple in the next suite along; Chloe looking for a bowl for me to be sick into. I hobble out of the room and into hers, expecting to find her awake and furious with me, but instead she is fast asleep, pyjamas and eyemask on, her clothes folded neatly on a chair in the corner. Whatever happened last night, it is abundantly clear that I was to blame; I was the one who fucked up. It was ever thus.

In a panic, I think about waking Chloe up to find out what happened, but even in my demented harpy state I know that this would not be a good idea, that I would only make things worse. I go back to my room and consider picking up the phone to reception to see if they can shed any light on what happened, but then I need to be sick again and I realise that after I have been sick, I desperately need to sleep. I shuffle across to the other side of the bed, where for the time being there is no vomit. I close my eyes and think I am going to cry, but nothing comes, just a strangulated sound of distress. This room is a mess. I am a mess. In my mind, the marathon does not even exist.

The drive back to London is awful, and not just because I spend most of it trying not be sick over Chloe's car. That morning I wake up some time before her, the thumping realisation of the vomit and the blood and the lump on my knee not just dawning on me but crashing onto me once again. Oh please free me from this. I strip the bed, bundle up the towels, try to scrub the sick off the carpet with some face cloths and shower gel. I have a bath, sink beneath the water and briefly consider not coming back up again. Eventually, I hear movement in Chloe's room and tentatively venture in to apologise and find out what happened.

I had expected Chloe to be cross with me. Yet again I had buggered up another nice, relaxing break. But instead she pats the mattress next to her and tells me to get in. 'Bryony, are you OK?' she says, a look of real concern on her face – something as rare as hen's teeth or me doing exercise. 'You were in a bad way last night.'

'I can tell. But I don't remember what happened. Are we being evicted from the hotel?'

'What happened was that you drank too much. We had that bottle of champagne. Then you ordered some beers and after that you suggested coming back here and doing shots. I was drunk; it seemed like a good idea, even though you had fallen down the stairs to the toilet. But then you did all the shots. And then you started being sick. I had to call the night porter because I thought you might be dying. He said he'd seen it all before and helped me get you into bed. You were sick on him, me and yourself. That sobered us all up. We put you in the recovery position and I sat up in my room reading and checking on you every twenty minutes until I fell asleep. How are you feeling today?'

'Oh great. I'm feeling on top of the world.'

'It happens to the best of us,' says Chloe, looking at me sympathetically.

But as we drive back to London, my stomach and mind churning in unison, I can't help but wonder if that is true.

For the next few days I am simply too busy to think about events at the country house hotel, let alone the fact that I have to do a marathon. This, as you know, is my best way of coping with things: create new worries and problems to subsume the old ones. We move to the new house. I stand in the doorway and look at the stairs – stairs! – that belong to us, and I pinch myself. Yes, I may be a 35-year-old woman who still drinks like a fifteen-year-old. Yes, I may spend a ludicrous amount of time talking to an invisible enemy I have called Jareth the Goblin King. Yes, I may not be able to drive. But on the plus side, I now own a house. Or at least part of the house, most of it belonging to the bank. Still, it's a start. And no matter how nerve-wracking the prospect of *Mad Girl* coming out is, I realise I have done most of the hard work. I have written the damn thing. All I have to do now is take it out there and talk about it. It is not my problem if nobody wants to hear about it, or read it. I have tried my hardest, and sometimes that is all that matters. As long as you do your best, the rest is all irrelevant, really.

Publication day, 6 June 2016. I wake up at 5 a.m. in my new house, surrounded by boxes, with the knowledge that today *Mad Girl* is available to buy in shops. Well, some shops. It's sitting there on the shelves, waiting to be picked up and read, and the thought TERRIFIES me. Why did I write about my bulimia? Why did I do that chapter on my rampant cocaine habit? Why did I talk about the abusive boyfriend, the one who slammed my arm in a door and then locked me in the garden until I stopped crying? He is still out there, and now he is going to kill me. WHY DID I ADMIT THAT FOR MUCH OF MY LIFE I I HAVE SUFFERED FROM AN ILLNESS THAT MAKES ME THINK I AM A SERIAL-KILLING PAEDOPHILE? People are going to back away from me at parties – that's if I'm still invited to any. I am going to be shunned by colleagues, friends and family. Oh God, my family. I gave my mum and dad an early copy a week ago and haven't heard from either of them since. Probably I will never hear from them again. And I will pass my shame onto my child, who will go through life known as the offspring of a freak. This was not what I planned. This is not what I planned AT ALL.

But it's too late now. I can't tell the publishers that I'll pay them back the advance if they pulp every copy. I can't call up my editor and say, 'SORRY, IT'S ALL BEEN A HUGE MISTAKE! YOU KNOW THAT BOOK I ALMOST HAD A BREAKDOWN WRITING FOR YOU? I MEAN THE ONE I DID HAVE A

BREAKDOWN WRITING FOR YOU? WELL, I DIDN'T MEAN TO WRITE IT! SORRY FOR THE MISUNDERSTANDING!' It's all out there now, in black and white, available for everyone to buy. Or not buy. Would that be worse? Oh God, what if nobody reads this book I had a breakdown over, the book that I don't think I want anyone to read? And I know I should be grateful that I have been published, that this is a good thing. But right now, in the fog of anxiety, OCD and self-loathing, all I can think of is how this good thing will turn out to be a bad thing. My head is very good at snatching defeat from the jaws of victory.

And yet as much as I would like to lie in bed ruminating over the disasters that are inevitably coming my way, I have to get up. I have to get up because Georgina, the publicist at the publisher, has arranged for me to appear on *Good Morning Britain* to talk about a mental health report which has found that the average time it takes for a young person in the UK to get proper treatment is a decade. 'They want you on in your capacity as a mental health campaigner,' says Georgina.

'A WHAT?'

'A mental health campaigner. That's how people are describing you now. Journalist, author, mental health campaigner.'

I laugh for about five minutes.

'Bryony, you are going to have to get used to this.

Eat, Drink, Run.

You've just written an entire book about mental health. People are going to start taking you seriously!'

I laugh for another five minutes.

But in the car to the *Good Morning Britain* studios, I am not laughing. I am sweating through my clothes, my top lip lined with a fine layer of moisture. Urggh, moisture. Even the word makes my stomach heave. When I get there it is not even 6 a.m. but already my adrenaline is racing. Already Jareth is up and at it, having feasted on a hearty breakfast of anxiety. I am taken in to a room where a nice woman plasters me in make-up and blow-dries my hair so that I look like I have walked off the set of *Dynasty*. By this point it is not even 6.20. Then I am pushed through into the studio where nobody seems to understand that the world is about to end. Cameramen, producers, runners . . . they are all going about their business as if today is a perfectly normal day. I am put on a stool behind a table where I realise I am going to have to discuss mental health with Piers Morgan. Piers Bloody Morgan. Why couldn't I have that lovely Susanna Reid? 'All OK?' he asks me, perfectly politely.

'Completely great!' I lie.

'Fab. Looking forward to discussing this with you,' he says.

I smile a rictus grin.

Then we are live, and everything is a blur. I feel like I might be the first person to spontaneously combust live on television. Oh God, can you imagine the head-lines on the *Mail* Online? 'Mad woman bursts into flames in front of Piers Morgan . . . and like a professional, he carries on to the next segment!' Or perhaps the sweat patches under my armpits will be on display. Maybe a boob will fall out of my top. Maybe, maybe, maybe . . . hang on, is Piers Morgan actually engaging me in a serious manner about mental health? Is he actually treating the subject with the gravity that it deserves? And am I actually talking to him kind-of-articulately about the reality of trying to get help for mental illness? Could it be that the two of us are talking on live television like *grown-ups*?

'It's important for us to be discussing this stuff openly,' I hear myself say. 'Because the more that we do that, the less able the government and people in positions of power are to ignore the crisis there is in mental health provision. That's why I do what I do. That's why I write about my mental health, in the hope that it makes other people feel they can talk about theirs too.'

I'm feeling kind of proud of myself. Passionate, possessed, pleased. Dare I say it, maybe this has even gone *well*?

'Well, Bryony,' says Piers, wrapping up the segment. 'I have to say that reading your columns always makes me feel better about myself!'

I knew it couldn't last.

'As do yours, Piers,' I smile, disingenuously. 'As do yours.'

That night, I do my first event promoting *Mad Girl* with an audience of readers. People stand up and tell me with tears in their eyes about their depression. A mother announces in front of 500 people that she feels she let her son down – her son who took his life the year before on his thirty-fifth birthday. I tell her that she didn't let him down – society at large did. A teenage girl gets up and tells me that her parents don't under-stand her, that when she tries to talk to them about how she feels they simply think she is attention-seeking. 'Your parents may not understand you,' I reply, 'but there are people out there who do.' I go home that night with a real sense that the dam has broken, that people are tired of suffering their misery in silence. It is a sense that only gets more profound as the summer goes on.

The longer that *Mad Girl* is out, the more I receive messages from people sharing with me their own stories of mental ill health. Increasingly I am being asked by people about how to set up a Mental Health Mates walk in their area. I am spending every spare moment of my time creating embarrassingly basic posters for new walks around the country that we can promote out on our new social media feeds – yes, Mental Health Mates now has its own social media feeds. Sensing that admin and organisation are not my strong points, a couple of the girls who came to the first walk offer to help me by creating a website and setting up an email account. Someone even suggests we look into applying for charitable status. By the end of the summer we have walks in Bristol, Newcastle, Leeds, London, Watford, Manchester and even an inquiry from someone who wants to set one up in *New York*. That this is becoming an actual real thing, that the crazy idea I had while out for a run back in January has somehow blossomed into something tangible and helpful is almost too much for me to comprehend. And speaking of running, I have done very little since the beginning of the year, unless you count the dashing around I am doing between engagements at which I have been booked to talk about mental health.

'How are you feeling?' says Chloe towards the end of the summer, when I meet her for a glass of rosé. Or ten. 'I'm feeling in need of another drink,' I say, drunkenly getting up to go to the bar and promptly falling face first into a hedge, ripping open the by now almost-healed wound on my leg that I managed to inflict upon myself back at that country house hotel in the Cotswolds. The gash bleeds and bleeds down my knee and onto my white Converse – it is so bad that the pub manager is summoned with his first aid kit to bandage me up. Looking like I have just been pulled alive from some rubble, and not like I have simply gone to meet a friend for a drink, Chloe helps me hobble towards an Uber who promptly refuses to let me in. 'You bleed on my seats, I pay lots of money for cleaning!'

'You can't make me walk home!' I cry. 'I can barely move!'

Chloe's head appears to sink into her hands. 'Is now a good time to mention the fact that you're supposed to be doing a marathon?'

4

To Ibiza

On 10 October 2016, also known as World Mental Health Day, three things happen in my world. The first is that I write a piece for the *Telegraph* announcing my intention to run the 2017 London Marathon in the hope of raising £10,000 for Heads Together. Ten thousand pounds. Am I mad? No need to answer that.

'Even being a slightly overweight mum with boobs the size of beach balls,' I write, perhaps slightly under-playing the 'slightly' bit, 'I know how important getting outside and doing exercise is to your mental health . . . This will most definitely be a huge challenge that I am sure will have some soaring highs and absolutely crashing lows. But when you compare it to some of the challenges people face in their heads every waking minute – right now, in fact – running the marathon is completely doable. It is more than that; it is the act of trying to turn a negative into a positive. It is worth huffing and puffing around London for five or so hours if in some small way it helps the people around us who struggle to breathe at all . . . I am doing this not just because I have fantasies of having a post-race pasta party with Prince Harry, but because in the last year I have had my eyes opened to the desperate amount that needs to be done to improve mental health provision in this country.'

The piece serves several functions, the most important of which is that I might actually start to take the prospect of the marathon seriously. If I don't do it now, having announced it in the paper and all over my social media, I will look like a prize twat. Also, by setting the fundraising bar so high, the part of my brain that is terrified of failure will do everything it can not to balls it all up. Even if I get terribly injured in training – which, let's face it, is entirely likely – I will crawl my way around that course. Even if I cross the finish line just as the London Marathon 2018 is about to begin, I will get to the end. If there is one thing I am very good at, then it is forcing myself to do something I really don't want to do by making myself feel bad.

The second thing that happens is that I am one of eight people doing the marathon for Heads Together who has been invited for a private meeting with the Duke and Duchess of Cambridge and Prince Harry, just before they appear at an event to launch a mental health first aid initiative at the London Eye. I'm not going to lie – when I see the invitation I wonder if everyone has taken leave of their senses altogether. The notion that I may be in any way worthy of these people's time not once but twice in the same year strikes me as utterly ridiculous. Standing in a large oak-panelled room on the banks of the Thames I am hit once more by the surreal turn my life seems to be taking. Having spent so long ashamed of my mental illness, suddenly it seems that I am not just forging a career out of it, but being lauded for it. For a moment, I dare to believe that the girl who felt she would amount to nothing might just be turning into something.

Ben from Heads Together appears and pierces my bubble by asking me how my training is going. 'Oh, you know,' I say, waving my hands around in the air, as if this might somehow change the subject.

It doesn't seem to work.

'I've done a few marathons,' says Ben. 'If you want any advice I'd be happy to give it.'

'That's really kind,' I smile.

'The first thing I would say is that as long as you can do 10k by Christmas, you'll be fine.'

'Oh yes,' I nod. '10k by Christmas. That's what? Three miles?'

'Six, actually.'

'Six. Easy! I can do that!'

111

Eat, Drink, Run.

'You can do anything you put your mind to, Bryony.'

'Do you think if I put my mind to it I could just disappear?' I ask, attempting to calculate the task in front of me.

'If you could hold off doing that for just a moment,' Ben says, nodding towards the door and the royals who have just stepped through it.

Within moments, the Duke and Duchess of Cambridge are in front of me. As I will soon learn, this lot don't mess about – they really do have places to go and people to see. 'I read your piece this morning,' says Prince William. 'It made me laugh. Especially the bit about beach balls.' I blush bright red. 'And if you get a pasta party with anyone, I reckon it will be with Prince George.'

'Great!' I burble. 'I'd love that! Can I bring my daughter? She's the same age.' Inside my head even Jareth is rolling his eyes in embarrassment.

'Have you started your training?' asks the Duchess of Cambridge.

'Well, you know.' I wave my hands in the air again. 'Soon!' I beam. 'Soon!' But all I can think is this: they really *have* read my pieces.

On the way back from the meeting, I check the comments underneath my piece online. I don't know why I do this – it's the equivalent of walking into a room and asking everyone there to list the things they hate most about you. 'You really must be mental if you think that you're going to manage a marathon,' writes one wag. 'Urggh, Bryony is so fat,' muses someone else. 'The thought of her wobbling round in Lycra is enough to put me off my breakfast.' And on it goes, each comment making me more determined to prove them wrong than the last.

Then I look at my email, and suddenly everything seems OK. By 10 a.m. readers have already sponsored me to the tune of £1,200. I am so flabbergasted that I almost miss the third thing that happens to me that day: the invitation from one of my editors at the Telegraph to start my 'fitness' journey at a boot-camp in Ibiza, for a big piece about beginning my marathon training.

Sure. I need to go to Ibiza. That's totally what I need to do.

Now I know what you are thinking. You're thinking: 'In the last chapter you were sick down yourself because you'd had too many shots. It ended with you being unable to walk properly after falling drunkenly into a hedge. The last thing you need, when you should be starting your MARATHON training, is to go to Ibiza, aka the party capital of the entire galaxy.' And you know, I'd be inclined to agree with you. All of those reasons you've just mentioned are exactly why I've never been to Ibiza. If I went there, I'm pretty sure I'd be one of those people who never leaves – I'd drop some sort of pill and get stuck on a permanent trip, raving away by myself in a corner of a superclub until eventually David Guetta would have to be brought in to evict me.

But this trip, I have been reassured, will involve absolutely no drinking of alcohol. And very little eating, if what I have read on the website is true. The Bodycamp bills itself as a 'luxury fitness holiday', the word luxury almost drowning out the fitness bit, but not quite.

'Imagine what a non-luxury fitness holiday is like,' I shudder to Harry, who thinks it is hilarious that I have decided to go to Ibiza for the first time to do a wellness trip – though in my mind it makes perfect sense, because if I'm going to learn to exercise I might as well do it in the warmth, with the option of legging it to a bar if it all gets too much for me.

'Have you read your "before you go" pack?' he asks, leafing through the hefty pile of papers I have printed out. 'Apparently you wake up at 6 a.m. and have a dance-off with your fellow Bodycampers. There's loads of hikes and boxing. You will also be eating delicious things like "mushroom bolognese on a bed of vegetable spaghetti". Sounds right up your street.'

'We should probably order pizza tonight,' I say, miserably.

At Heathrow Terminal 5, I sit down and weep. By rights I should be thrilled that I am going to sunny

Ibiza at the end of October, just as the weather is starting to turn grim here. But in reality I am terrified. I am terrified of what the other people on the trip will be like – there is no way I will have anything in common with a bunch of people who are willingly *paying* to eat vegetable spaghetti for a week – and I am terrified that I will humiliate myself horribly in front of them. I am a (by now) 36-year-old woman who drinks and smokes too much and can't go three days without a double bacon cheeseburger. How am I going to survive on a diet that is 80 per cent plant-based, especially when I will be spending all day exercising? My tiny yomps around Clapham Common could hardly be classed as strenuous physical labour. Yes, I found them hard. But when you are as chubby as I am, even walking to McDonald's is hard. For all my talk and bluster about the importance of exercise, the reality is that I have hardly done any since I was in the grips of an eating disorder in my early twenties, when I would go spinning twice a day until I could barely stand up. My relationship with my body is such an appallingly abusive one that the thought of confronting it, of dealing with it, fills me with absolute dread.

The packing list has done little to reassure me: swimming costumes for 'sea sports' (what, no sunbathing?), painkillers (ibuprofen is preferred, apparently), blister plasters (sexy), two-litre Camelbak. I have to Google what this is: a backpack that enables you to carry liquids around when you are in the wilderness and out of reach of a tap, apparently. The thought appalls me. 'I don't like to be any more than ten metres away from hot and cold running water!' I shriek to Harry one evening, over yet more rosé. 'It's *uncivilised*, like being asked to take the night bus home instead of an Uber!'

'Bryony,' Harry says, shaking his head. 'Only you could make a luxury fitness retreat sound like you're going into the jungle to be fed critters by Ant and Dec.'

'That's an unfair comparison,' I huff. 'They get paid tens of thousands of pounds to do that AND they get a night in the Versace hotel afterwards. But this, THIS is just for the goodness of my own personal wellbeing!'

'Honestly, would you listen to yourself?'

I tell my editor that I will give it four days, instead of the full seven that is recommended. 'I guarantee you that by then I will be completely broken and battered and probably in need of hospital treatment,' I announce, in a not entirely undramatic fashion.

'I bet you will be begging to stay,' she smiles.

'Bet you a Mars Bar I won't.'

'Deal.'

So here I am at the airport with my Camelbak and a suitcase full of cheap workout gear that I bought the day before at TK Maxx, because that is the only place that seems to stock workout gear for fat people. There is also a sports bra I ordered from a specialist website for the larger lady, a place I would previously have avoided for fear that it was a haven for perverts.

As I wait for the gate to be announced, I sit in Pret a Manger working my way through a mac and cheese. It is 9 a.m. After that I have a smoked salmon and egg breakfast baguette, followed by a brownie. I've never really had a sweet tooth – a relief because if I did I would be at least four stone heavier – but knowing that sugar is out of bounds during my stay at the Bodycamp is enough to send me headfirst into the pile of chocolate-covered goodies at the counter.

After this, I may be full – but I am by no means finished. I consider buying some black-market crisps to smuggle away in my luggage for when hunger strikes during the week, but even I know that is cheating. If I'm going to do this, I might as well do it properly. Instead I decide to buy a couple of bags for the flight.

Once I have boarded the plane with my stash of cheese and onion delights, I settle down for a blissful couple of final hours filling myself with salt and fat. Two mouthfuls in, I am rudely interrupted by the arrival in the seat next to me of a tall, thin, blonde girl who looks like she has walked off of the pages of *Sports Illustrated*. She smiles at me with pearly white teeth. I grin back, salt and pepper and grease and flakes of crisps all over my face and chest – I make a mental note to forage in my bra for scraps should I get hungry later. 'I'm Jo,' she says, holding out an immaculately manicured hand. I wipe mine down on my leggings so as not to cover her in grease too. 'I'm Bryony,' I say.

'You're not by any chance going to a bootcamp, are you?' she asks, doubtfully. 'It's just that I am and the people there said they had booked me on the flight out next to someone else who was coming and . . .' She notices my bag of crisps and I can see in her face that she thinks she has made a terrible mistake. 'Sorry, how embarrassing. As you were!'

I grin really widely now, aware that I probably have mashed crisps in my front teeth. 'Actually,' I say, 'I am going to bootcamp! Sorry, you get to spend the week with me. Well, not exactly the whole week. I'm doing a piece on it for the *Telegraph*, I'm a journalist you see, and so I'll only be there for four days, because I thought that was probably about as long as any of you could bear with me! I mean, you're probably all superfit and healthy and I'm' – I wave my bag of crisps in the air – 'well, I'm not! I like crisps. And alcohol. And cigarettes. And—'

'I like crisps and alcohol and cigarettes too,' says Jo, dreamily. 'Could I have one of yours please?'

'Oh, I don't have any cigarettes on me right now, sorry. Plus you're not allowed to smoke on planes.' I shuffle around and realise my arse is almost too big for the seat.

'I meant one of your crisps,' says Jo.

'Oh, right, sure, of course!' I look into the empty

bag. 'It appears I have eaten them all. Oops!' I have a brainwave. 'I could always see if I have dropped any down my cleavage if you're really hungry? There's usually something down there.'

Jo laughs. 'And there I was worrying that everyone was going to be really boring,' she sighs, and settles back in her seat.

Sometimes it's good to remind yourself that although people might look different on the outside, we are all a seething mass of insecurity on the inside. Fat, thin, tall, short . . . self-doubt and fear will fit itself into any shape or size. That evening, upon arriving at the Bodycamp's villa, I have all my preconceptions about people blown away; I meet the model who is trying to switch career, the businesswoman trying to get over the suicide of her boyfriend, the mother who has been crippled with post-natal depression, the teacher trying to make friends after moving across several continents from Australia, the dad who is drinking too much and wants to change his ways. As we sit around the vast table where we will eat what exists of our meals it occurs to me that the only things I have to be frightened of this week are the limitations my brain has spent so long setting for me. Nobody here is out to get me – everyone here is after the same, elusive, thing: we all want to feel better.

The Bodycamp is run by a brother and sister called Kate and Ben, and their friend Rick, a former Royal

Eat, Drink, Run.

Marine turned fitness trainer. Once we are all there they go through the rules with us. I brace myself for a litany of miserable instructions, and am surprised when I hear none. 'No mobile phones when we are eating,' says Kate. 'We want you to be focusing on your food, not Facebook. No alcohol, obviously. All we really ask of you is that you just turn up every morning. Turn up, hand yourselves over to us, and prepare to have fun.'

The next morning I am woken by the dulcet tones of Nina Simone's 'Feeling Good' blaring through the villa. I suppose it's one way to deal with your version of the Black Elephant or the Black Slug. I jump out of bed with Kate's words ringing in my head, and pull out some 'workout' gear from my suitcase. It all looks so uncomfortable, so unforgiving, so unnecessary. I squeeze myself into the leggings and grimace at the unsightly layer of flab that seems to spill over the waistline. Next comes the sports bra, which I soon realise is an item of clothing that requires a degree in engineering to put on. It has six clasps at the back, none of which I can manage to fasten. 'Think on your feet, Gordon,' I say, realising I have broken two nails just trying to put the garment on. 'Think on your feet!'

I grab a towel and creep across the hall to Jo's room. I knock on her door. She answers in a crop top and tiny shorts. 'My God,' I gasp, rubbing my eyes. 'I want to leave my husband for you.' I rub my eyes again. 'Am I still allowed to say things like that?'

'Good morning, Bryony!' she beams, and then notices the towel I am wrapped in. 'You look . . . well. Can I help you with anything?'

'As it so happens you can.' I take her arm to lead her across the hall back to my room, and in the process drop my towel and flash my boobs at her. She pretends she hasn't seen – though given the size of my boobs, it's entirely likely I have flashed the entire villa. 'Oh God,' I say, scrambling with the towel. 'I'm so sorry. Listen, I know we only met yesterday and that we barely know each other. But I need you to help me put my sports bra on. You know those Victorian corsets that they have in those period dramas?' Jo nods. 'Well it's a bit like that, and I'm having a wee bit of trouble getting it on. You're the only person I feel comfortable enough with to ask to help me into it.'

Jo nods again and follows me to my room. I pick up the sports bra and her eyes widen in . . . what, exactly? Shock? Horror? *Wonder*? It is a feat of engineering to marvel the pyramids and Stonehenge. 'OK, we can do this,' she says, a look of pure concentration on her face. I flop my boobs into the bra, wriggle around so nothing is hanging out, and hold each side of the fastenings in the hope she can get them together. 'OK. Breathe in,' she says. 'One, two—'

'ARGGHHH!'

Eat, Drink, Run.

'And you're in!'

As I stand and look in the mirror, I realise it is quite possible that my bra is actually obstructing my airways. 'It's . . . cute,' Jo says kindly, although we both know that 'cute' is no way to describe the material monstrosity that appears to cover me from my neck to my ribs. 'If this was PVC I could totally wear it to Torture Garden,' I manage to breathe.

'I don't like the sound of Torture Garden,' says Jo. 'But I think this bra' – she is doing finger quotation marks as she says the word bra – 'will definitely do the trick when it comes to keeping you secure this week.'

'That's if I can actually breathe in it.'

'No pain, no gain!' chirrups Jo. It is not even 6.30 a.m., and already I feel like I have gone several rounds with Mike Tyson.

My first task of the day is to have a weigh-in with Rick, who ushers me into a room and tells me to stand on a machine that looks like it belongs in an episode of *Star Trek*. This machine will measure my visceral body fat, my muscle mass, my bone mass, my basal metabolism, my height, my weight, my BMI, and my hydration levels. I swear that the only thing it can't do is see into my soul – which is good, because if it could it would know that I have a deep hatred for it. Wearily I step barefoot onto the machine and close my eyes in the hope that when I open them I will discover this has all been a terrible dream and I am actually a lean, mean fighting machine with nothing to worry about. 'You could run a marathon right now if you wanted to,' I imagine Rick announcing. 'You're the fittest person we've ever had here. I could get some tips from YOU!' Instead all I hear is the beep and whirr of the machine as it passes its judgement on me.

'Is it terrible?' I say, before Rick has even had a chance to look at the piece of paper that is being printed out the backside of the machine.

'We don't use language like that round here,' chastises Rick.

'I only said "terrible".'

'Terrible is a terrible word. Nothing is terrible. It's all just stuff we can improve on.'

'OK,' I say, looking at my toes. 'But is it terrible?'

'I'm not answering that. Now sit down.'

I do as I am told. Rick hands me a small book in which he staples my measurements. I look at them, but they don't mean much. Not that I need to understand them to know that they are all *terrible*. My visceral fat is exceptionally high. Rick explains that not all fat is bad – in fact some of it is pretty good for you – but the visceral stuff is. It's the fat that contributes to heart disease, dementia and cancer, amongst other things. I am not nearly hydrated enough and I lack muscle. I am not just overweight – I am obese. My metabolism is so slow that – as I suspect will happen during the marathon, that's if the marathon happens at all – an elderly woman in a rhino costume could overtake it.

'Want to hear your metabolic age?' asks Rick.

'Not really,' I reply.

'It's fifty-one'

'What the actual fuck? There must be some mistake! Maybe you read it wrong and it's actually forty-five?' I'm clutching at straws here.

'No, fifty-one,' says Rick matter-of-factly.

'Does that machine tell you how long you have left to live? Is it weeks?'

He stares silently at me.

'Is it days? Tell me if it's days, and I will get on the first flight home so I can spend my final hours with the ones I love.'

'Next,' shouts Rick, and then Jo is on her way in to stand on the machine of doom, which tells her she has a metabolic age of nineteen.

Of course it does.

'Comparison is the thief of joy,' announces Rick, as we settle down for our first session. He is pacing in front of us, taut, toned and tanned. I'd fancy him if I hadn't just found out that I was about to die. 'You're going to be tempted to hold yourself up to the other people

124

while you are here. DON'T. Everyone is different. If you can't do a pull-up you can do a squat. If you can't do a squat you can jog on the spot. There's something for everyone here whatever the ability.'

We nod at him like terrified children on our first day of big school.   'Now,' he continues, 'just a few things I want to make clear. I don't want to hear you say "I can't". You always can. There will be no whingeing that you're TIRED. What you are is RECHARGING! Nobody is to complain that their muscles are sore. Instead, you are feeling SEXY! Got that?'

We nod quietly.

'I SAID: DID YOU GET THAT?'

'YES!' we shout, somewhat startled.

'You're not tired, you're . . .'

'RECHARGING!'

'You're not aching, you're feeling . . .'

'SEXY!'

This is going to be a long four days.

First off, we have the bleep test, which takes me straight back to school. Just in case you have erased it from your memory in an attempt to ease the trauma, I will remind you of what it entails: running back and forth between a set of bleeps that get quicker and quicker, to prove how fit you are. They use it in the police force and the army. Its sole purpose at school seemed to be to dispose of any self-esteem I had left; of course, it is entirely possible that it wasn't *all* about me, even if it felt that way as I stood panting in the gym hall, unsure if I would ever catch my breath again.

Standing there by the side of a pool in Ibiza, I can't help but be pissed off that at the grand old age of thirty-six, I am being made to feel inferior again. Surely I should have grown out of this by now? Surely the fact I own a house and have a job and a husband and a child means I don't have to put up with this bullshit any more? And yet as Rick makes us line up, none of this counts for anything. I am a child again – I may have a metabolic age of fifty-one but emotionally I feel about three. Everything I have ever achieved – every article or book I have written or battle against Jareth I have fought – seems to mean nothing here, where I am being measured exclusively on the amount of fat suffocating my major organs and my inability to run as quickly as possible between pips.

'Are you ready?' asks Rick. We nod our assent. 'I SAID: ARE. YOU. READY?'

'YES!' we roar as one, and then we're off, and I'm doing OK, or at least until pip three when I get a bit overexcited, slip over, and land flat on my fat – but crucially cushioned – arse.

Later that day, we play a game of touch rugby and I end up with a black eye. I tell myself it is better than

ripping open my knee drunkenly in a hedge. I devour
the chicken broth and the tiny morsel of roasted black
cod with pak choi and spring onions that comes with
a couple of flecks of 'wild' rice. Idly – and it's the only
thing I will do idly this week – I wonder what non-wild
rice looks like – is it studious? Does it read books?
Like early nights? – but my stomach is churning so
eagerly at the thought of more food that I soon have
to stop. I drink what feels like three gallons of water
and spend a great deal of time peeing. I learn how to
do something called a burpee, which seems to involve
squatting down, throwing your legs back, and then
jumping back up again. Burpees look simple, fun even,
but do not be fooled. They have actually been sent
from the third circle of hell to punish those of us who
have committed the cardinal sin of gluttony. I discover
I am so unfit that I cannot even pull myself up into
a sit-up, but that if someone stands on my toes it all
gets much easier. I rip my leggings bending down to
lift a (very small) weight, and realise I have only packed
one pair. Kate goes and finds me a leopardprint set,
which makes me look like Bet Lynch attempting to
do squats behind the bar of the Rover's Return.
Speaking of which, even if we were allowed booze, I
wouldn't have the energy to drink it. I laugh so much
that my belly aches, though that could just be the
exercise. I turn up. I tune in. I give it my best. And
so it is that I go to bed wondering if maybe, just

127

maybe, I should change the flight and stay for the full seven days.

On Monday morning I wake for the 6.30 a.m. 'stretch' class to discover that I cannot even stretch myself out of bed. I am suddenly aware of every muscle in my body. They are screaming at me in pain. Abductors shriek. Abdominals wail. Glutes howl. But Jareth is suspiciously quiet. Jareth, I reckon, is knackered. He's had no booze to feed him, no junk food to nurture him. He's spent a day battling endorphins, and for the time being he doesn't seem to have the energy for the fight. He's asleep – for now – and I'll take that. I need to get ahead of him; I need to produce some more endorphins to go to war with him.

I remember Rick's instructions from the day before. I am not aching – I am feeling SEXY. I am not tired – I am RECHARGING. I wrap my towel around me and head to Jo's room so she can put my sports bra on, then I squeeze myself into the leopardprint leggings and throw on a T-shirt from Adidas. In the mirror I nod at myself – this is a definite improvement on the woman who ten months ago had terrified innocent dog walkers by galloping around Clapham Common in a *Star Wars* T-shirt. Downstairs I am secretly pleased to learn that everyone else is aching, too. We lie flat on mats and make various grunts and growls as we lengthen calves and backs. With every bend and stretch

I imagine ridding myself of the bad energy that Jareth has spread through my body for so long – then I berate myself for sounding like a hippy.

Breakfast is a tiny cup of granola that we are allowed to pour some almond milk on – obviously dairy is banned here. We are allowed one mug of cold-pressed coffee a day which seems to excite everyone but me. 'Oh, I don't drink caffeine,' I say, smugly, neglecting to add that this is usually because I am so hungover every morning that I cannot bear the thought of putting more toxins inside me.

As I make my few flecks of granola last, we are told what we will be doing for the day. A morning of boxing, followed by a 'mystery session'. I am excited by the idea of boxing, if only because I assume that, being a 'larger' lady, I might have a bit more brute strength behind me. But I have confused brute strength for visceral fat, and I spend the morning weedily punching pads and trying not to fall over as some bird-like crea-ture with flowing locks lands the kind of punch on me that I like to think would floor Muhammad Ali.

Perhaps my lack of strength is because I am not concentrating. All I can think about is the mystery session and what it might entail. Skydiving in forma-tion? Abseiling down a cliff? Synchronised swimming? After a roasted squash and feta salad lunch, we are told: our mystery session is a dance lesson. My stomach plunges, my blood runs cold. I think I would prefer to take my chances with the skydiving. Nausea spreads through my body: I will the roasted squash and feta not to come back up – after all, there's no more where that came from.

'Are you OK, Bryony?' asks Jo. 'You look very pale.' I nod quietly, and contemplate just how much I hate dancing, how self-conscious it makes me feel. School discos were such a trial that downing a litre of cider and spending the evening throwing up in the bogs always somehow seemed preferable to having to do the Macarena. While friends enthusiastically lined up to do the dance to Whigfield's 'Saturday Night', I could be found in the corner drinking vodka out of a water bottle. The idea of dancing in unison always struck me as so embarrassing, so mortifying, like having to watch your parents kiss or hearing the bed creak upstairs as your flatmate has sex with their boyfriend. From a very young age, when I flatly refused to do ballet despite the teacher telling my mum I had the 'perfect' feet for it, I knew it wasn't for me – but then that might have had more to do with the leotard stuck up my bum than any of the actual movement involved.

I think that my hatred of dancing might be part of the reason I took so many drugs in my twenties – that and the fact that getting wasted was one of my very favourite things. If I was wasted then I could truly lose myself – I didn't give a shit what anyone thought. I remember Chloe repeating to me the old adage that you should always dance like nobody is watching. My reply would inevitably be: 'Well, in that case, you are going to need to get me an E. Or perhaps some coke.' I was no more prepared to dance than I was to walk naked down the street or admit to fancying my geography teacher at school. And now they are asking me to do it *sober*, in front of a group of people who two days ago were strangers to me? I don't think so.

'Tune in, turn up,' I hear Kate say in my ear. 'You might even like it.'

I don't know about that, but I am beginning to get the impression that I don't have much of a choice in the matter. I also know that if I don't do it, I will be missing out on the chance to produce some much-needed endorphins that will help me fight Jareth. And wouldn't he love to see me fail? If I sit out the dance class, wouldn't I just be giving Jareth much-needed ammunition?

And at that moment, I know what I have to do.

I have to dance.

The instructor is a tiny pocket rocket of a thing who appears not to have stopped moving since she was born. A former backing dancer for Madonna, every move that Ali makes is with the grace of a cat. I, meanwhile, finally feel something of a kinship with my Black Elephant. How could I have been so cruel to it when all along it only ever felt like I did on the dancefloor? I feel a tinge of sadness for the Black Elephant, then pull myself back into the room as soon as Ali tells us that we will be learning a dance routine to the tune of Beyoncé's 'Single Ladies'. It's like all my worst nightmares come true.

Ali says that we are going to start with some free-styling – truly, words to drive dread into the heart of any sixteen-stone woman with a metabolic age of fifty-one. Freestyling, explains Ali, will involve all of us dancing to the song freely for a few minutes, so that we can 'get our groove on'. I think I might actually hyperventilate at the sound of these words. She walks to the back of the room to press play on her iPhone, which is plugged into a giant speaker. We all look awkwardly at one another, as if she has just asked us to take off all our clothes and writhe around on the floor. 'All you have to do is dance!' Ali squeals, as if reading my mind. 'All you have to do is have FUN!'

Fun? Fun is drinking bottles of rosé in the garden while smoking fags. Fun is going to Byron for a burger and cheesy fries. Fun is sitting on the sofa watching Netflix while your husband rubs your feet. Fun is a lie-in. Fun is a long, hot bath with a good book. Fun is NOT freestyling to Beyoncé with a bunch of strangers. But it's too late to run away. The music is striking up, and slowly everyone is actually getting into it.

I stand like a stone, silently taking in the sight of

eight people 'getting their groove on'. It feels horrifying to me. It's not that they are bad dancers – it's not even that I am watching their dancing. It's the overwhelmingly awful realisation that I am going to have to do something completely outside my comfort zone. I think I might cry. As Ali takes my hand and starts to spin me round the room, I realise that I actually *am* crying.

What is going on? What is happening to me? Ali tells me to just follow her, to just copy her, to just *go with it*. I take a deep breath and do as I am told. What's the worst that can happen? I wonder, and realise that this is a question I have posed to myself an awful lot of times in the last few months – and that I am probably going to ask to myself a whole lot more in the coming months.

I find myself twirling, and wriggling, and writhing. With tears in my eyes, I join in. I get my groove on. I go with the flow. I follow Ali and my fellow Bodycampers. I notice that everyone else is focusing intently on what they are doing – that nobody could give two hoots whether I can dance or not. They're all too wrapped up in whether or not *they* can dance.

Chloe's words return to me, and suddenly it becomes clear to me. I didn't need to take the E, or snort more coke. I didn't need the cider or the vodka, or to hide in a corner. All along, I had the power to dance without any of these things. I had the power, because in actual fact, nobody *was* watching. Not at the school disco,

133

not at the club, not anywhere. Every time I set foot on a dancefloor, I wasn't being judged as if I was in an episode of *Strictly*. People weren't ready to score me, to make cutting remarks to me about my ability to wiggle my hips or turn elegantly. Looking around the room, I realise that the world doesn't revolve around me. I don't need to be self-conscious. I can dance however I want to dance, and nobody will care. They'll just be happy that I am there with them, tuning in, *turning up*. That is enough. That will always be enough.

'You are so sexy when you lose yourself in dancing,' Ali tells me at the end, holding my hand. 'You have no idea how much power you have in there, and what you could do with it.' I go upstairs, change my flights, and make a mental note to remind myself that quite often, doing the thing you really don't want to do is the best thing of all.

5

To What Feels Like The Ends of The Earth

When people ask me now how I went from being someone who couldn't run for a bus to someone who could do a marathon, my answer is that I didn't. Nobody does. First I went from being someone who couldn't run for a bus to someone who would jog very slowly for fifteen to twenty minutes, then I went from being someone who could jog very slowly for fifteen to twenty minutes to someone who spent an entire summer throwing up over themselves, and then I went from someone who spent an entire summer throwing up over themselves to someone who was packed off to a bootcamp in Ibiza by a kindly editor who could see I might need some help.

Eat, Drink, Run.

I used to think that change, when it happened, was a sudden thing, a volcanic eruption or an earthquake that shook everything up as if from nowhere. If I read enough lifestyle magazines and started enough fad diets, then all I had to do was lie back and wait for it to drop into my lap, in the form of my dream job or my ideal man or the perfect penthouse suite. Change, when it finally came, would be sudden, sharp, speedy, a bolt from the blue that would make everything better. And in the meantime, I could just shuffle on through my life without actually . . . well, changing. In the dictionary, change is described as an act or process through which something becomes different, but in my mind I had confused it for an act or process through which something becomes fixed.

It was halfway through the thirteen-mile hike up an Ibizan hill that took place towards the end of the Bodycamp when I realised that I had never actually been interested in the concept of change. All I had ever wanted was a cure-all, a magic panacea that would solve all of life's ills – when I was depressed I wanted the psychiatrist to make it better by upping my dose of antidepressants; when my mind felt like it was on an intensive washing cycle, I hoped that a twenty-minute run would switch it off. I wasn't a bad person for wanting these things. I was just an ill one who desperately wanted to feel well again, even if my attempts at wellness were fickle and fleeting and got dropped the moment I felt better.

I don't think I was ever alone in this. Exhausted by the seemingly neverending battle with mental illness, who doesn't yearn for the quick fix, the diazepam that blots out the anxiety, the burger full of calories, but most importantly comfort? It had never really occurred to me that food had served as toxic a purpose in my life as cocaine or bad men, that I had alternately picked it up and put it down as a way of getting high – not until my control over it got taken away from me that week in Ibiza. But attempting to clamber up that hill, my body fuelled only by goodness, my mind was suddenly clear and focused. I knew that change, if it was going to last, if it was going to really make a proper difference, was going to have to be an intricate and ongoing process. It was not going to be as simple as visiting the Bodycamp for a week and returning a completely different woman. Sudden change, I realised, is as precarious as an ill-thought-out attempt to overthrow a government. One minute all the signs are there for a fresh start; the next you're back to being beaten black and blue by the old regime.

Standing there, my heart hammering in my chest and my lungs feeling as if they were going to collapse, I knew very suddenly that I had a long way to go – both literally and metaphorically – if I was to even get to the London Marathon start line. While my fellow Bodycampers had happily forged ahead and were now atop the hill eating their mid-morning protein snack,

Eat, Drink, Run.

I was crying somewhere near the bottom with Jo, who had taken pity on me and was doing her best to motivate me beyond the tears. 'Everyone is rooting for you,' she said, and while I knew she meant it to sound encouraging, I could only hear it as patronising. I felt humiliated and pathetic. I was seven miles into a bloody *walk* and already I was ready to give up. How was I going to make it through an entire marathon?

It was then that I had my epiphany. I realised I didn't have to make it through an entire marathon – at least not that day. All I had to do was make it to the tree five metres to my left, and then to the boulder five metres after that. I just had to get to mile eight, and then to mile nine, and so on and so on. It didn't matter if it took me all day – I had my trusty Camelbak, and if that failed I had Jo's enthusiasm to get me through. I took a deep breath and started climbing. All I had to do was put one foot in front of the other, and remember not to look down.

Two hours later we were back at the villa and I was in a hot bath counting the blisters on my feet. Eight in total, nine if you counted the one that had evidently burst somewhere around mile ten. I had done it, that was all that mattered, and now I was on the home run. Indeed, one round of boxing and two swimming races later I leapt on to the machine that could see everything except for the insides of your soul, where I discovered that I had lost eight pounds in weight, gained significant muscle mass and gone down one point on the visceral fat scale. My metabolic age was still fifty-one, but I figured you're only ever really as old as the girl who is helping you into your sports bra, and given that Jo's metabolic age was closer to nineteen, there was still hope.

At Heathrow airport, I expected my husband and daughter not to recognise me; I fancied that Harry would faint in shock at the sight of his newly hot wife. But he just said, 'You look well,' followed by 'Pub tonight?', and then Edie told me we were going to Nando's for lunch. I may still have looked like a chubby caterpillar to them, but it didn't matter. All that mattered was that I knew that inside, there was a beautiful butterfly waiting to come out.

So this is how I go from being the girl who could barely climb up a hill in Ibiza, to the girl who did 10k before Christmas.

I go straight to Nando's, followed closely by the pub.

I know, I know. This is not exactly classic marathon training. But I need to be realistic. I am no more going to cut out booze and nice food until next April than I am going to abstain from watching reality TV or brushing my teeth. If I were suddenly to become a clean-eating freak, my will to be good all the time would break within four days, a week and a half tops. I would be right back to where I was pre-Ibiza, all that visceral fat strangling my organs and my weight nudging ever closer to seventeen stone. I need treats – I just have to earn them. 'So we are going to a pub that is a half an hour walk away,' I tell Harry. 'No Ubers! And tomorrow we are going to walk the entire perimeter of Richmond Park so Edie can see the deer. Then I'm going to cook us some sort of lentil or quinoa dinner.'

'Righto,' says Harry, looking a little suspicious, not to mention green around the gills.

Of course, on this I have to be realistic too. It's not that I can't cook – it's that I don't cook. I think that it's because I don't have the time, but in reality it's just because I don't have the energy, my body sapped of enthusiasm and motivation by the carbohydrate-dense lunches I shovel down my gob at my desk every lunch time, dessert a generous helping of whatever it is Kim Kardashian has been up to that day via the *Mail Online*. By the time I have picked Edie up from nursery, got her bathed and in bed, the last thing I feel like doing is whipping up some super-healthy salad that is heavy in nutrients and light on calories. Does that sound fun to you? I mean, if it does, you're probably reading the wrong book. You probably should be over there making chocolate mousse out of avocado. To me it sounded like misery, like coming home and having to chow down on some weeds from the garden, topped perhaps with a few snails. A delicacy somewhere, sure, but not where I lived in south London.

Here we had supermarkets selling ready meals, hummus, kettle chips and – were I to crave some vegetables – carrot batons helpfully shaved down for you. We had Deliveroo, aka the greatest culinary invention since sliced bread or the Nespresso machine. Why bother going through the effort of 'cooking' something second-rate when I could simply download an app, order some stir-fry from people who could actually cook, and be done with it?

But, like the dancing and the hiking, I was willing to give it a go. Plus, making my own food would give me more of an incentive to eat it 'mindfully', as I had been taught at Bodycamp – which is to say slowly and contemplatively, instead of manically.

My first attempt at lentils was not successful. 'It looks more like something you'd serve up to a cow on a farm than a meal, per se,' said Harry. He was right; it was awful. My second attempt, at quinoa with chicken and vegetables, was marginally better, but only because I covered it in olive oil and salt. On the third day, Harry told me to stop what I was doing – he had discovered that Waitrose sold pulses and legumes, as they are officially known, in easily microwaveable packages. All I had to do was not make a hash of the meat and vegetables I intended us to have on the side, and to promise him that every Friday night we would eat at Byron.

*

Eat, Drink, Run.

Slowly but surely, the marathon begins to take over my life – and the lives of everyone who has the misfortune to have to spend their waking hours with me. I bore everyone at work with the discovery that I 'pronate', meaning that my foot rolls slightly when it hits the ground.

'I had my gait analysis done at the weekend in the local running shop,' I tell Eleanor, the girl who sits next to me at work. 'I bought these amazing trainers that will help make it better.' I don't tell her how much they cost – bloody hell, running gear is expensive. She surveys the hot chocolate and biscuit in my hands. 'Gosh, that's *fascinating*,' she says. 'Would you like me to tell you about what happened when the plumber came to look at our boiler last week?'

After a while, I start turning up to work in sports gear. 'Well done! Did you run to work?' asks my colleague, Joe.

'Oh no, I didn't run,' I say, shaking my head. 'I just thought I would start wearing all the gear so I *feel* like a runner. Like method acting, if you will.'

'Right,' says Joe. 'You're the Daniel Day-Lewis of marathon running, then?'

'Joe, that is SUCH a good analogy. Thank you. That is exactly who I am right now.'

He nods. 'And there I was thinking that the best way to feel like a runner was to actually run. But what do I know, eh?'

'Do you think,' adds Eleanor, 'that when this is all over, we'll all get medals too?'

I ignore their sarcasm. I am a blooming flower, a ray of light, a walking, talking paean to positivity. I start to buy running magazines, and learn about things such as hill sprints, interval training, and long runs. Who cares that as yet, I have not attempted a single one of them? Just *knowing* that they exist makes me feel like Paula Radcliffe.

I learn that people training for a marathon should do strength and conditioning work, such as Pilates. Jo, who has become a friend since Bodycamp, tells me she will take me to a class. 'There's this brilliant type known as Reformer Pilates,' she explains to me. 'You basically do it on a bed, with lots of ropes and pulleys to help you get into the various positions.' Exercise on a bed? That sounds good to me.

But arriving at the Reformer Pilates class, I realise that all is not as it seems. This bed, which I had imagined to be comforting, enveloping and supportive, actually looks like something out of *Fifty Shades of Grey*. It is a medieval instrument of torture; it is the kind of thing I would expect to see in a dungeon, not a respectable gym offering introductory memberships for just £39 a month. And looking at the lithe frames of all the other women in the class, I suddenly feel really self-conscious. As I climb onto the bed, I try to remember what I learnt on the dancefloor

– that the world does not revolve around me, that nobody else in this room could care less if I were taking part in the class wearing a ballgown and high heels. An hour later, Jo has to pull my legs out of the stirrups, which I seem to have got stuck in. My hips feel as if they have been stretched to the point of snapping. 'My husband would love one of these at home,' I joke, but nobody seems to laugh. They are too busy warming down, a process I am discovering is absolutely essential if you don't want to spend the next two days walking like Peter Crouch doing the Robot.

As I book myself into next week's class, I realise that the marathon is a bit like being pregnant again – I feel like I am the first person in the world to do it. But just like being pregnant, I am not the first person in the world to have done it, and so it is that everyone has advice for me. Buy supplements. Drink protein shakes. Stretch morning, noon and night. Make sure your name is on your shirt on the day, so people can shout encouragement. Use energy gels – but try them out before the big day, as at first they tend to go straight through you (nice). Cover yourself in Vaseline to prevent blisters. Eventually, all your toenails will fall off. Can someone remind me why I am doing this again? Oh yes. Heads Together. Mental health. Charity. But most of all, the advice was: run, run for your life.

Which reminds me. At some point, I am actually going to have to get moving.

Learning to run is really as simple as putting one foot in front of the other. But being able to do it for any length of time is a little more complicated than that. I download a Couch to 10k app – and then panic when I realise that a marathon is 42k. Jesus sodding Christ. 'Forty-two kilometres!' I scream at Harry that day. 'Forty-two! At the moment, I can't even run one!' He is just pleased that I finally seem to have grasped the enormity of what I am doing. Breathing deeply, I tell myself not to think about the other 32k right now – that can come later. Today, I just have to get outside and move.

At first, I feel like an infant learning to walk. I keep tripping and stumbling as ligaments, joints and muscles creak into life, as if for the very first time. The app features the annoyingly robotic voice of a woman who I imagine to have long, swishy, sex hair. You know the type: pulled up into a perfect ponytail that can be thrashed around wildly during particularly energetic and acrobatic lovemaking. You know: the kind of hair I don't have, the kind of sex I am not having (but maybe I will start to have if I follow the woman's instructions?). As I listen to her directions – walk for one minute, run for thirty seconds, and so on and so on, until you want to throttle her and scream 'EASY

Eat, Drink, Run.

FOR YOU TO SAY, CHILLING OUT THERE ON YOUR PERKY BACKSIDE INSIDE MY IPHONE!'
– I try to paint a clearer picture of the anonymous woman who is, right now, the only thing between me and the nearest pint of lager. Resent her as I might, I have to admit that without her, I wouldn't have the foggiest what I was doing. She is, in many ways, my guardian angel, my guiding light, and I should probably have a bit more respect for her.

Firstly, I decide to give her a name – I imagine that she's called Kimberley, because Kimberley is exactly the kind of spunky, sassy name that a woman with swishy sex hair who can run 10k would have. 'Morning Kimberley!' I say, every time I press start on the app, and who cares what anyone walking past me might think. Right now, I need Kimberley. Without her friendly, warm encouragement – 'you're halfway through your workout!' – I would almost certainly give up after fifteen minutes.

What's more, I am beginning to realise I actually like her, on account of the fact that, day by day, she is getting me that little bit stronger, and helping me to run for that little bit longer – one minute, then two, and now three. I certainly prefer her to Jareth, who seems to be in a coma. I yearn to hear her robotic pleas to 'start walking!', and occasionally find myself yelling 'THANK YOU KIMBERLEY' into the air, a little louder than I had intended thanks to my noise-cancelling headphones. I even tell myself that if the worst comes to the worst, I can just walk/run the marathon – all that matters is that I don't get a cab round it. But as the weeks go on, I notice that Kimberley tells me to walk less and less. Eventually, I realise she has stopped altogether, and that I am ready to do my first 10k. It is 22 December, just before the Christmas deadline that Ben from Heads Together set me.

I mean, would you look at that?

On the day I plan to do my first 10k, I have a giddy feeling inside me. I initially think it's because it's Christmas Eve tomorrow, but then I realise that it's actually nerves and excitement that have come with the thought that I am about to attempt something that just two months ago seemed impossible. I am about to run for one hour twenty minutes, which is how long I have worked out it is going to take me based on my speed – or should that be my slowness? I know the average time for 10k is closer to fifty minutes, that some people could walk faster than I run, but then I tell myself that the average runner isn't overweight with boobs the size of small planets strapped to their chest. All those tall, rangy men who smugly sprint past me in the park – *they* should try doing that with a pair of tits. Furthermore, aren't us slow runners, the ones who are on our feet for double the time, the *real* elites? It's not as if I am working any less hard out there – in fact, by going slowly,

Eat, Drink, Run.

I am making things harder on myself by dragging it out.

That day, I ask the babysitter to come at 4 p.m. so I can do my 10k. At 3 p.m., I start to mainline water as if it is going to run out – Ben from Heads Together told me that I shouldn't weigh myself down with unnecessary water bottles, only the essentials. At 3.30 p.m., I put my swanky new running leggings on – I know they are swanky because the shop assistant referred to them as 'tights', which is how all the pro runners speak. These tights promise to sculpt my thighs and make my muscles work harder than normal leggings – then again, at £75, I'm hoping they might take out the rubbish too. Honestly, it amazes me how much 'sportswear' costs – I've seen Victoria Beckham turn up on the front row in dresses that are cheaper. I try to remember that however frightening my high-tech 'tights' seem, running is essentially a sport that can be done on the cheap, in a *Star Wars* T-shirt and a ratty pair of Converse if needs be, and that I am only investing in this to support me through the marathon. All I really have to do is put one foot in front of the other, I tell myself, again and again and again.

Once the tights are on, I wrestle myself in to my sports bra – I don't even have to ask the babysitter, now that's progress, folks! – and throw on a top, throwing on a top being exactly the kind of thing that Kimberley would do (no way does she chuck one on, or put one on). Then I zip on my waterproof running jacket, an item of clothing that makes me cry on account of the fact that it cost close to the amount I used to spend on an entire outfit from Topshop. 'But it's just an ANORAK!' I said to the exasperated shop assistant. 'Why does it have to cost so much?'

'Because', she sighed, 'it has sweat-wicking fabric that cools *and* warms you, depending on the temperature, as well as keeping wind and rain off.'

'Does it have an inbuilt hairdryer for when I get caught in a downpour?'

'It has a hood, madam, if that's what you mean.'

'No, I meant a hairdryer.'

'Madam, if you don't want the coat can I kindly—'

'I'm joking! I want the coat. Give me that coat. Together, we are going to run miles and miles.'

The shop assistant doesn't look convinced.

But now it's on me, and I'm ready to go. I just need the isotonic energy gel that I have been told by marathon experts to try before the big day. I've read that you don't really need gels until you are running half marathons, and 10k is basically half of a half marathon, so it is not essential. But to me, 10k seems such a ludicrous distance that the gel serves more of an emotional crutch than it does a physical one. Just knowing it is there to use in case of an emergency instills in me a sort of comfort. After all, I won't have Kimberley today. If you love someone, you have to set them free – and I need to know I can run the distance on my own. Goodbye

Eat, Drink, Run.

Kimberley, goodbye. You have served me well, but now it is time for me to let you take your robotic voice and swishy sex hair to someone else who needs it.

I let in the babysitter, and say goodbye to Edie. She asks me where I am going. 'Are you going exploring?' she says, pointing at my anorak – sorry, running jacket. 'You look like you are going exploring.'

'I'm going running, darling.'

'You are always running now,' she says, shaking her head. 'Is running your job, mummy?'

And I realise that, for the next few months, that is exactly what it is.

It is dark by the time I get going, which is exactly how I like it. In the dark, nobody can see me wobbling around the common like a weeble. In the dark, I don't have to pay any attention to those super-speedy men who I feel so inferior to. I have another app on my phone, Map My Run, that will tell me how far I have gone and how long it has taken me. With my energy gel in one of my many pockets (is that what you are paying for? Pockets?), I set out at what I think to be a respectable pace. Then a bloke speed-walks past me. I try to ignore him, carry on. At one kilometre I am out of breath and my lower back aches – at a set of traffic lights I take the opportunity to stop and stretch myself out. But I tell myself I just have to do that another nine times, and suddenly it doesn't seem so bad.

I put on some Beyoncé, move to the beat, wonder if I am becoming one of *those* people – the ones who go for a run because they want to and not because they feel they have to. It was my choice to come out here and run on a bitterly cold, dark afternoon the day before Christmas Eve, when I could have been tucked up inside with my daughter watching *It's a Wonderful Life* or one of the other schmaltzy films that are on 24/7 this time of the year. I could have put it off – indeed, eight or nine weeks ago I would have put it off, so much so that I would never actually have got round to doing it. But here I am, and would you look at that – three kilometres done. Another fifteen minutes later and I'm at five. Halfway! Time for the gel? Why not? Treat yourself - it is Christmas after all!

I open the packet and swallow down its sickly sweet contents, which give me an immediate boost. Map My Run tells me my pace has picked up, and I'm feeling good. I'm feeling confident. I'm feeling . . . oh God, I'm feeling like I need the loo. My stomach is growling and grumbling, my bowels apparently twisting inside me. The gel! Those damn marathon experts were right! The only problem is, I am in the middle of a common. The only loos nearby are the public ones in the children's playground, and I wouldn't want to go to those in the light, let alone the dark. I might never come out again.

I run up and down on the spot. I am quite literally trying to think on my feet. I know! I know! There is a pub about 200 metres away if I sprint across the common and skip the paths. If I can just get there, it will all be OK. I start to propel myself forward, hoping against hope that the motion might ease the sensation of throbbing in my bowels somewhat. It doesn't. In fact, it makes it worse. If I am not quick, I am going to shit myself. I am actually, genuinely going to shit myself, and in my new 'tights' at that. Perhaps that is why they are so expensive? Perhaps they act like nappies and absorb up to 50 per cent more 'waste' products than other, cheaper 'tights'?

Unwilling to find out, I sprint across the grass, wondering if all those super-fast blokes were actually just trying to get to the loo and the look of smugness on their face was something else. Hey – it's something to make me feel better the next time I encounter one on my travels. Closer and closer I get, the warm lights of the pub honing into view. I'm nearly there, I'm nearly there, I'm . . . I'm running through something unmistakeably soft, squishy and very, very smelly. Whatever it is has come from a bottom – thankfully, not mine. Or does that make it worse? I don't have time to think. I run towards the pub, in through the door, and then into the loos. Once on the toilet seat I relax – but only momentarily. An investigation of my brand-new trainers finds that they are covered in dog shit. I laugh, do my business, and then go about cleaning my shoes with loo paper, soap and water. When I am done I look at my phone and see I only have 2k to go. Two kilometres! No amount of dog shit can bring me down!

I leg it out of the pub and continue on my way. A text arrives from the babysitter. 'We've gone to Byron for burgers!' I work out that Byron is probably two kilometres away. I sprint there, and as I run through the door I tick over into 10k. 'I'VE DONE IT!' I shout at the surprised babysitter and my daughter, who is slurping on a milkshake. 'I'VE BLOODY DONE IT!' Then I sit down, and a funny thing happens.

I order a salad.

That night, I ask the babysitter to stay on after I have put Edie to bed, so that I can go to the pub with Harry and celebrate. 'I ran 10k!' I say, over and over again as we walk there. 'I ran 10k!'

'Did you mention you ran 10k?' says Harry. 'Or that you're running a marathon?'

'Just because you've never run 10k!' I say, taunting him. 'You're just jealous!'

'Maybe I am,' he smiles, as we walk into the pub. 'And I am proud of you. Just one thing: this doesn't mean you can have a pint and a fag for every kilometre you've run, OK?'

'Au contraire, mon cherie,' I smile, turning my attention to the barman. 'Au contraire!'

On Christmas Eve, I wake with a curious mixture of both a throbbing head and body. It is a hangover – but not as I've ever known one. 'It's like my brain is competing with my thighs to see which one can cause me the most pain,' I say. 'Though strangely, I think the thighs are currently winning. Is this what it feels like to be healthy?'

'I'm not sure Mo Farah celebrates every 10k with a piss-up at the local pub,' Harry says, passing me some paracetamol and ibuprofen. 'So no, I don't think this is what it feels like to be healthy. I think it's what it feels like to be . . .'

'A healthy hedonist! That's what I am! Oh God. That makes me sound like such a wanker. I hate myself. And now I have to do battle with the hordes and go out and get the last of the Christmas presents. Thirty-six years I've done this, and I never learn.'

'It's better than last Christmas,' notes Harry, 'when you were waking up with terrible OCD and no way of dealing with it. You've come a long way in twelve months, remember that.'

He's right. But I have a little further to go before the year is out. Five miles on Christmas Day, and another 10k on New Year's Day, because I feel absolutely invincible. 'You're actually going to do this, aren't you?' Harry says to me, as I jog into the house on the first day of 2017, just as everybody else is coming round from their hangovers. And I am. I *so* am.

6

Back to the Olympic Park

At mile eleven, I discover chafing.

In truth, I don't know what is weirder: the sight of the skin between your thighs after running eleven miles, or the very fact that you have just run eleven miles.

Probably, the latter.

I had heard about the chafing, obviously. People had told me about it, warned me that when fabric met heat, skin and sweat over a long period of time then friction would occur. I had been informed about the bleeding nipples that tend to befall marathon runners. Given mine are the size of small side plates, I didn't much like the sound of that. But like getting painful wisdom teeth and tearing open in childbirth, I had just hoped it wouldn't happen to me. I'd get lucky. I'd be one of those women – those women being Kimberley, I imagined – who could run for miles without so much as a sore toe.

Of course, experience had taught me otherwise. I still had the scars on my feet from the hike I had done back in Ibiza. But I had hoped that perhaps that was just an aberration, a one-time thing, much like almost-shitting myself after downing that gel. In all my long runs since – my God, I was now going on weekly long runs every Sunday, as well as three small runs during the week – my bowels had remained steadfastly intact. They barely flinched when I drank the isotonic mixture that would keep me going for another half an hour. And so it would be with chafing. I was now immune to it, surely. Like a vaccine, I had experienced my mini shot of it on the hike all those months ago, and now I was fine. My skin would remain silky smooth and sore-free, and scientists would want to analyse my genetic make-up to see how I managed it.

My second 10k was easy, so the next weekend I jumped up to eight miles (12.8k). That, too, made me feel nothing but high. I had gone out early one rainy Sunday morning in January and run down to the river where my £150 anorak had protected me from the elements, and returned feeling as if I could run not just eight miles, but the world. It amazed me that I could produce that feeling with my own body alone. I soaked in a long bath and went for a long lunch, smug in the knowledge that I was training for a marathon without falling apart. As well as that, *Mad Girl* had gone straight to number one in the bestsellers charts. I felt like I was finally turning a corner. My regular training updates in the *Telegraph* were showing me the kindness of readers, and my fundraising target was going up at an astonishing rate. Emails were coming in from people telling me all about how exercise helped them, and how they hoped it would help me. A card came in the post from a man who thanked me on behalf of 'couch potatoes and depressives everywhere', including his son who sadly had suffered from the illness for most of his life. Out of it fell a cheque made out to Heads Together for £10,000. I was flabbergasted by how generous people were being, especially after so long feeling so alone. If I needed any encouragement to get out there and run, then I had it in spades in the messages and donations I was receiving from readers and people who followed me on Instagram.

The Bryony who never does anything by halves had reared her manic head again. The training programme I had printed off the internet cautioned taking it easy and only upping each week by increments of a mile but I felt that I was on fire and, anyway, what did the stupid training programme know about my body's capabilities? Me, the woman who did not chafe even though everyone else did. I decided that the next weekend I was going to go for double digits. Get ahead of myself. 'Bank some miles in my legs,' I tell Harry, pompously, this being the kind of thing I had read experts say in running magazines.

'Are you absolutely sure that's a good idea?' he replies, as if he knows better than me, the woman who does not chafe. 'After all, you know what they say . . .'

'What do they say, oh running expert who hasn't actually done any running since I met him?'

He narrows his eyes at me. 'It's a marathon, not a sprint.'

Like the messages from trolls telling me I am too fat to do this, his words of caution only make me even more determined. I call up Jo, who has been telling me for some time that she wants to join me on a training run. 'This Sunday, 9 a.m. Me, you, and a ten-mile run.' She agrees to come with me.

'As long as I don't have to put you in your sports bra again.'

'I can do that sports bra up with one finger now, baby.'

'Good to know.'

When Jo arrives at my house, she lets out a gasp. 'You've lost so much weight!' I'm hearing this an awful lot at the moment, and I'm not going to lie – I like it. For all my posturing about being happy with my larger size, I am realising that I am far happier feeling fit and healthy, that being able to wear jeans again has its benefits – namely, they don't tend to rip quite as often as ASOS leggings. I can sling Edie on my shoulders without doubling over, and carry her upstairs to bed without feeling I need to stop halfway. I could run for buses if I was actually taking them – but mostly I am walking everywhere, to increase my time on my feet.

We set off. It is a beautiful day in late January – almost, I realise, a year since I had the idea for Mental Health Mates. Now we are all over the country, and the week before there was a meet-up in New York. Someone in New Zealand has been in touch to say they are interested in doing one there, too. Kat, Denean and Polly, some of the people who came to the first walk, are now helping me with all the admin and set-up, and I realise as Jo and I run down to the river through Battersea Park that for the first time in my life, I feel supported in my mental health. I hope they do, too. It seems remarkable to me that through the simple act of reaching out, things can feel so incredibly different. As we run along the river, I start to plan our one-year anniversary walk.

The sun shines bright as we make our way past Battersea Power Station, up towards Millbank. At Westminster we have done five miles, and I am feeling jubilant. We keep passing other runners who smile and wave, and again I feel a sense of fellowship. I feel less alone. Past the London Eye we go, up to the Tate Modern, over the Millennium Bridge towards St Paul's, and all the while I am hit by the beauty of London, and how grateful I am that I am here, moving through it, rather than back in my bed with the Black Elephant and Jareth. Neither of them are with me today. Even the voice of Kimberley seems distant. It's just me, my legs and my will to power forward. Six miles, seven miles, eight miles, nine. By the time we get to Tower Bridge, we have run ten. 'Let's just keep going a little bit longer,' I say to Jo, ignoring the exhaustion in my bones, and the rubbing feeling between my thighs. Map My Run announces we have done eleven miles. We finish, get a cab back to mine, and it is then that I realise that I am the woman who *does* chafe.

One long, hot bath later, and I am rummaging through the First Aid box for something to help the delicate skin between my legs. To be blunt, it looks like I have been masturbating too much; it looks like I have been flayed. Vaseline? That probably would have helped *before* I set out for the eleven-mile run, but right now it feels a little like the horse has bolted. Bog-standard moisturiser is going to hurt. I stare down at the tube of cream I haven't used since Edie was toilet-trained. There is nothing for it but nappy cream.

I slather the thick, medical ointment between my legs and let out a moan of pleasure. It is, without doubt, the nicest thing I have experienced in that particular area of my body for some time (marathon training seems to be playing havoc with my sex life – perhaps it's because as soon as I put my head on the pillow I pass out in exhaustion). I am a 36-year-old woman walking around covered in nappy cream, but I don't care. It's the simple things, after all. And I couldn't be happier.

The next day I hobble out of bed, slather myself in more nappy cream, and check my email. Would you believe it: there's another invitation from Ben to hang out with the royals, this time at a marathon training day event back at the Olympic Park. I read it to Harry, who shakes his head in disbelief. 'I am wondering who is really mental here: you, or the guys at the palace who keep inviting you to hang out with the people who will one day rule over us. Seriously, this is what, the third time you've met them?'

'The fourth, actually. There was the Christmas party I got invited to at Kensington Palace where they poured champagne out of magnums of Mumm and I asked a waiter to just stand next to me with his magnum, so that he could constantly refill my glass. It was almost as if I was being WORSHIPPED!' Harry shakes his head some more. I originally didn't want to put that story in this book in case you started to think I was showing off, or name-dropping.

'OK, the fourth. I mean, the royals are really going above and beyond the call of duty here. I know it's their jobs to be charitable to members of the public, and I know that you're a complete charity case. But isn't this going too far?'

Eat, Drink, Run.

'I really can't help it if you're jealous that I'm spending so much time with a man called Harry who isn't you. But really, would you listen to yourself? He's got a girlfriend! It's OK! You don't have to worry about me running off with him!'

More head shaking. 'I take it back. You're not a charity case. You're a headcase.'

As I arrive at the Olympic Park for the training day, it strikes me just how much has changed since the last time I was here, ten months ago. Back then I was coming down off a weekend of taking diazepam, a gibbering wreck who could barely hold it together. Now I feel calm and confident, a little bit more like I belong, thanks to the marathon training and the expansion of Mental Health Mates. I make my way to the training ground where our day is due to take place, all of the Heads Together runners meeting for the first time. It's inspiring to see so many of us in the same place, all of us different shapes and sizes but with the same motivation: helping to break the stigma surrounding mental health.

Ben from Heads Together is there. He pulls me aside and tells me what is going to happen. There will be a running coach who will take us through some drills that will help us with our training, and a few talks from people who are expert runners themselves: Paula Radcliffe, no less, the women's marathon record holder, and Iwan Thomas, the Welsh sprinter and former European and Commonwealth Games champion.

'Then the Duke and Duchess of Cambridge and Prince Harry will arrive, and there will be a relay race in which a few of the Heads Together runners will take part. One of those runners is you. You're on Prince William's team.'

I look at Ben in a puzzled manner. 'Say that again?'

'There's going to be a relay race. Three teams, headed up by the Duke and Duchess of Cambridge and Prince Harry. They will each have three people on their teams. You're on Prince William's. We'll be filming it for the news. It's going to be great fun.'

'It's going to be great fun,' I repeat.

In disbelief, I am introduced to two other Heads Together runners who will be taking part in the relay: Sian Williams, the news presenter and marathon runner who has just recovered from breast cancer, and Sean Fletcher, the *Good Morning Britain* host who will be running to raise awareness of OCD, which his teenage son also has. 'Well, this won't be humiliating,' Sean says, but he is one of those tall, rangy men who I suspect runs really fast. Sian, too, has done umpteen marathons, and though she is a tiny slip of a thing, currently it's me who is feeling incredibly small.

The royals arrive and we are split into our teams. It turns out that Prince William will be passing the 'baton' to me, so to speak, and that I will be on the leg of the relay against Paula Radcliffe and Iwan Thomas. 'I think there's been some mistake,' I say to Prince William. 'Either that or you have drawn the short straw.'

'No, no,' he says politely. 'I have big hopes for you, Bryony.'

We take our positions on the track. We only have to run fifty metres but as I stare down the lane at Prince William, who is gently ribbing his wife by pretending to push her out of the way, I realise that the entire distance is lined on one side by cameras, all ready to capture the moment the young royals reach their team mates. I gulp hard. No biggie. It's not as if my humiliation during *It's a Royal Relay* is going to end up televised around the world. No sirree. The crowd starts to count down. 5, 4, 3, 2, 1 . . .

And suddenly, the three young royals are running towards me. As my heart thumps in my chest, I wonder if I have ever had a stranger Sunday morning. Prince Harry speeds ahead of his brother who, I realise, is veering out of his lane. Just who the hell does he think he is? But given my running form, I don't feel I am in any position to criticise – I will just have to let it lie. Before I know it, the Duke is racing towards me. I position myself perfectly, ready to high five him as I have been told I must do by Ben. But in all the excitement, and all the veering out of lanes, that does not happen. Instead, the heir to the throne accidentally slams into the side of my body, just as I watch the Duchess of Cambridge gracefully high five Paula Radcliffe, like a woodland sprite or a beautiful fairy. Trying not to gasp, or shout out in pain, or laugh – after all, it feels like a million cameras are trained on me – I start to run. Was I just accidentally winded by Prince William? Would this be the sum total of my achievements, when I talked to my grandchildren in years to come? And was this going to end up on the evening news? It didn't really matter. As I tried to propel myself up the track to Sean, I realised that I had been left in the dust by both Paula and Iwan. When I reached Sean, I sent an embarrassed smile down the track to Prince William, who was gamely willing his more able team members on. 'It's the taking part that matters,' says Sian, when she reaches me, and we fall about laughing.

Later, Ben from Heads Together asks if a camera crew can film a short interview with me and Sian, focusing on how we are feeling about the marathon. After the humiliation of It's a Royal Relay, I feel I can take on anything. (I have already started to receive texts from friends commenting on my snail-like pace.) We stand in front of the cameras and start to chat. 'This is going to be your first marathon since recovering from cancer,' I say. I put my arms around her, noticing tears in her eyes. 'It's OK to get emotional.'

Eat, Drink, Run.

Sian laughs. 'Don't start me off. There's a camera there.' What Sian hasn't seen is that there is also a Prince Harry there, hiding just behind a cameraman, watching us as we are filmed. Inside I have this crazy idea – not my first, and probably not my last. And as I am fast learning, crazy ideas sometimes make the best ideas. If you don't step outside your comfort zone, you don't know what is possible. I take a deep breath, and make a split-second decision to put my plan into action.

'I think Prince Harry should come in and give you a cuddle' I say, motioning at the then fifth in line to the throne. The camera crew shoot each other awkward looks. Prince Harry himself appears a little taken by surprise. But then he steps forward, takes his place in front of the camera, and throws his arms around . . . *both of us.* 'I'm going to give both of you a cuddle,' he smiles, as Sian and I process what is happening. 'It's amazing,' he beams. 'It's exciting stuff!' In the background I giggle nervously.

'It IS exciting,' says Sian to Prince Harry, 'and nerve-wracking. And I think the thing is that we both do it for our mental health, and if we don't run, we are particularly miserable.' Prince Harry nods along.

'I keep saying that this is going to be really, really hard. Really tough,' I say. He appears to be listening intently. 'But it can be no tougher than the days when you have the crushing weight of depression on your chest and you can't move at all. I feel that this is a real gift.' I am in full flow now. 'And to be able to show people who maybe right now don't feel like they can leave the house – well, a year ago I couldn't leave the house, but here I am, having a chat with Prince Harry.'

He smiles softly. 'You've got that experience,' he says, rubbing his chest. 'When you're pushing through the miles, well, this is nothing compared to what I've been through.'

'Yes!' we beam, in unison.

'People with mental health issues are the perfect candidates for marathon runners,' it suddenly occurs to me. 'We're very good at demon-wrestling.'

'We need to tie all of you together,' laughs Prince Harry, and maybe it's my imagination, but the look of recognition on his face gives me the impression that when he says 'you', what he actually means is 'us'. That 'We' that Carson McCullers spoke about all those years ago.

Running is boring. There's no doubt about that. Running on a treadmill, in particular, is a special kind of tedious, the kind that makes you wonder if you might have accidentally died and woken up in purgatory. I try to avoid it at all costs, on account of the fact that I won't be running the actual marathon on a treadmill, so why waste my time training on one?

Eat, Drink, Run.

Outside – where there are birds and trees and police cars giving chase to whatever gang fight has gone off on the streets of Lambeth – is, if not exactly fascinating, then at the very least more engaging than staring at a computer screen on which the miles tick by agonisingly slowly.

At first, I listened to music, because that's what everyone who runs does, right? It's just a given, and I would always rather that than be stuck with the noise in my own head. But then I found that the fast-paced music I was listening to was putting me in serious danger of doing myself an injury. I was trying to run to the beat of a dance track, and it wasn't doing me any favours. Plus, my headphones kept falling out. I also had a Fitbit by now – the perfect gift for the obsessive compulsive who has everything – and that could track how far I was running instead of my phone. Being able to go out with as little as possible on me pleased me – it made me feel like I was somehow going faster, even if I was still only marginally quicker than the Black Slug.

So now I really was stuck with the horrors inside my own head . . . except, there didn't seem to be any. Try as I might, I couldn't find Jareth anywhere in my brain. It was like he had downed tools and stormed off in a huff, aware that he was no longer being fed the self-loathing he lived for. In his place was the curious sensation of . . . well, nothing. Just *boredom*.

And I kind of liked boredom, compared to the stuff that had been there before. I kind of liked it, because out of boredom came imagination, and out of imagination came some of the best fantasies I had ever had. After a while, running became like dreaming.

It was amazing where my brain was going to on my runs, the places it was travelling to in order to avoid the pain of the chafing every time my thighs rubbed together, or the twinge of a hamstring that wasn't entirely down with how far I was pushing it. When I was out on my runs, I realised that I was daydreaming for the first time since I was a teenager, and I loved it. Frankly, given the bizarre and fantastical direction my life seemed to be taking, what with royal relays and hugs from Prince Harry, was it any wonder? My mind was coming alive with magic instead of misery. I was no longer Bryony, the fat bird with crippling OCD. I was Bryony, the woman who was training for a marathon, the woman who could do anything she put her mind to. For the only time in my life, more than getting married or becoming a mother, I felt transformed. I felt, I guess, like a new woman.

In the pub one night, I tell this to Chloe. She stares at the pint on the table in front of me. 'If you're so much of a new woman, why are you still smoking then?'

'Because, Chloe, I need to keep it real.'

'By giving yourself emphysema?'

'Do I sound like I have emphysema?' I cough.

Eat, Drink, Run.

'I worry that you're pushing yourself too hard. Running endlessly, still coming to the pub with me, getting up at the crack of dawn with Edie . . . You might feel like a new woman right now, but I bet you tomorrow morning, when you wake up with a hangover, you're going to feel like more of an *old* woman.'

Chloe may not believe me, but right now I don't care. The next morning I do wake up with a slight hangover, but I decide that the best way to get rid of it will be to go for a jog. 'If in doubt, run it out' has become my irritatingly chirpy motto of late. I swear that if I had met myself a year ago, I would have taken a bat to me.

I set off from the house and head towards the Common, the one I could barely get around a year ago without hyperventilating. I feel chuffed with myself. I feel so chuffed that I decide I am going to do an epic run, a ten or eleven miler. My tight pockets are crammed with gels and a bank card in case I collapse and need a cab – or, less dramatically, a bottle of water. I can do this, I think, even if I'm not supposed to be doing this in the middle of the week so soon after my last long run. What could possibly go wrong? I ask myself yet again. I trot along, and go into full daydream mode.

From miles one to three, I am in Los Angeles, where I have been sent to interview Poldark. I know that's not his real name, and I know that I'd probably be more likely to be interviewing him in the Cornish Lizard than Los Angeles – but bear with me, this is pure fantasy. As I arrive at the interview in a sumptuously appointed suite of the Beverly Hills Hotel, I notice Poldark staring at me. Perhaps he is admiring my new, marathon-svelte figure, all fourteen stone five pounds of it? I smile seductively, and then remember I am a married woman who should know better. I conduct the interview in what I hope is a professional manner, despite being aware that he is flirting. Can he not see the ring on my wedding finger? At the end of the interview, he sidles up to me and slips a piece of paper in my pocket. When I arrive back in my room, I open it and see his phone number written under the words: 'Call me, Poldark'. Just as I am trying to process my shock, my own phone rings. It is Harry, back in London. Has he a sixth sense? Does he know I am about to stray? No, he is just calling to tell me that he has been diagnosed with a rare condition which means he can never be intimate with another person again. 'I'm so sorry,' he says, 'but I just want you to know that while I will always love you, I would hope that you find someone else who can meet your other . . . needs.' I hang up, call Poldark's number, and have insane sex with him for days on end. The chafing is obviously not an issue in this fantasy.

From miles three to six, I am winning the London Marathon. Nobody can believe that this girl who couldn't run a few months ago is now in with a chance of beating the elites who have been training all their lives. 'It's incredible,' gasps Steve Cram, as the event is televised live on the BBC. 'I can hardly believe that just a few weeks ago I was beating her during a royal relay race,' says Paula Radcliffe. 'I always knew she had it in her, that girl.' As I cross the line in just under two and a half hours [forget that this is how long it takes me to run twelve miles – remember, we are in fantasy land right now], the royals wait with my medal, covering me in hugs and holding me aloft in congratulations. The next day, every front page features my face alongside the adoring Duke and Duchess of Cambridge and Prince Harry. Shortly after that, it is suggested that I try for a place in the Tokyo 2020 Olympic team. Through my new publicist, I release a statement to the world's press. 'While Bryony is flattered by suggestions that she may be of Olympic standard, she would not want to take away from the considerable efforts of the athletes for whom Tokyo is their life's ambition. She has decided instead to focus on her writing, and her charity work.'

From miles six to nine, I am being interviewed on *The Graham Norton Show*, alongside actors starring in the Hollywood adaptation of *Mad Girl*. 'How does it feel to have Jennifer Lawrence playing you?' asks Graham, but before I can answer, Jennifer – or Jen, as I have come to know her – has come in and started talking. 'I just wanted to say that it has been SUCH an honour to play such an inspirational woman, and I am so, so grateful that we have become such good friends over the last year or so. And I'm so delighted that she has asked me to be godmother to her and Poldark's new baby! Can you believe how quickly she's got her figure back?'

Between miles nine to eleven, I am hanging out with Prince Harry, and we are getting along famously. 'Hey Bryony,' he says, 'I'd just love it if I could give you an exclusive interview about mental health. I really want to talk about my experiences of it in the hope of helping others, and I can't think of anyone in the media I trust more!' I take his hand and look seriously at him. 'Are you sure, Harry?' I say. 'I don't want you to do anything that you are not comfortable with.' He hugs me again, we sit down, and do a groundbreaking interview that wins him plaudits and me the Pultizer Prize. The *Telegraph* give me a massive pay rise and tell me that from now on, I can write what I want. Finally, we can afford to do the loft extension, not to mention the side return.

At the finish, it occurs to me that while most of this is absolute first-class fantasy, some of it might be rooted in reality. Given that the palace keep inviting me to meet the royals, given that I am running the marathon for their charity, given that they seem to trust me, is it really that ludicrous to imagine that Prince Harry might give me an interview about this subject that is clearly so close to his heart? OK, it might not be groundbreaking, it might not be revealing, but it could help a lot of people, to hear someone so high profile talking in depth about the reasons him, his brother and sister-in-law chose to get behind a mental health campaign. I could pitch it as two people getting their heads together to talk about mental health.

It was funny how my mind, so hopeless and low a year ago, now seemed so active and enthusiastic. It was just following my body, I suppose, which was showing me each week that it could do a little bit more than it could the one before. Right then, the realms of possibility when it came to mental health seemed endless to me. It felt like there were no limits to what this campaign could achieve. I called up Jason, the man in charge of public relations at Kensington Palace, and nervously burbled my idea down the phone to him.

'Well, I can most certainly ask him,' Jason replied, and I felt so excited that I did a little jump, followed by a yelp as pain shot down my right thigh.

7

To the Doctor's Surgery

My next run is hardly a run at all – more of a shuffle, hop and step before I realise there is something very wrong with my right leg and turn back. 'That was quick,' says Harry. 'You really are upping your pace if you managed to do five kilometres in five minutes.'

'Please don't joke,' I snap, before collapsing on the sofa in pain. The tears follow shortly after.

My thigh feels as if it is on fire. From my knee to my hip, it throbs. The sensation is so sharp, so nasty, that it makes the chafing feel like an orgasm in comparison. Harry makes me prop the leg on the coffee table, and then disappears into the kitchen. He reappears with a frozen bag of peas, which he tells me to put on my thigh. 'Do not move,' he implores. 'I know what

I am doing. When I did my Duke of Edinburgh back in 1992, one of the other boys slipped and fell down a muddy bank and we learnt that you immediately have to abide by the ICE rule: ice, compression, elevation. If you do that then there is minimal damage.'

'The thing is,' I whimper, 'I think I might have done this a couple of days ago and kind of ignored it. I think I might have been injured for some time.'

'Oh,' says Harry.

'What's wrong, Mummy?' asks Edie, sweetly. 'Do I need to get my nurse's kit?'

'I think it might take more than that,' I sniff through my tears.

The next day, I hobble down the road to my nearest physio. I didn't even know I had a nearest physio until yesterday – my need for one up to this point in my life had been so minimal that I'm not actually sure I knew what a physio was. A person who cracks your back? No, that was a chiropractor. Someone who sticks needles in you? No, that was an acupuncturist. A human with an uncanny and almost magical ability to predict the future? No, that was a psychic, and right now, if I saw one of those, I fear they wouldn't have anything good to say other than: 'I see for you a long, sedentary life on the sofa.'

As I sit in the waiting room, I feel terrible – physically and mentally completely wrecked. All that bravado, all that believing I had known better than the experts . . . look where it had got me. Pride most definitely comes before a fall, and I was proof of that, even if I hadn't actually fallen. I'd just worn myself down with my own overenthusiasm. I had got ahead of myself. I hadn't respected my body, or any of the advice from the people who actually knew what they were doing. How could I have thought that I was going to be the first person to train for a marathon who could do it *their* way and get away with it? I was my own worst enemy. I kept on remembering all the times I had cockily asked myself what was the worst that could happen to me. Well, it turned out that the worst that could happen to me was me.

It occurred to me very suddenly that what I had been doing was exercising obsessively compulsively. I thought Jareth had gone because he was no longer taunting me with thoughts that I might be a serial-killing paedophile. But he hadn't gone – he had simply taken a different form. As ever, he had just manifested himself in the thing that happened to be the most important to me at the time – and right then it was the marathon.

Miserably, I handed over my credit card to the woman on reception, who charged me £85 for whatever it was the physio was about to do to me. I would have emptied my bank account if it meant they could make me better. 'Sorry, Harry, we can't afford to pay the heating bill and there will be no electricity for a while, but on the plus side I am now fighting fit and ready to run a marathon.' Exercise had become as important to me as the very basics I needed to live.

I was ushered into a room that featured diagrams of the human body and its muscular system. A skeleton hung sadly in the corner, as if to say, 'Look what you have done to yourself.' I sat and stared at it, awaiting my fate.

It turned out that the physio was a tall, handsome French man who announced almost immediately that he was going to have to have a good feel 'around ze affected area'. But even that couldn't cheer me up. He left the room while I removed both my trainers and leggings and got on his examination bed, pulling a towel over me to protect my modesty. When he returned he told me to motion towards the area that hurt. I did. 'You do not mind me feeling around here?' he asked. 'I can get someone to watch if you are uncomfortable.'

'It's fine,' I said irritably, keen for him to get started. 'Just make me better.'

Slowly, Frenchie the physio felt his way around my right thigh, and then my left one for comparison. I realised I hadn't done my bikini line for a while, and surmised that what with all the chafing, that particular area of my body probably looked like a war zone, or a bombed-out forest, the type you might see in an episode of *Game of Thrones* or a documentary about Chernobyl.

Obviously, he'd seen a few, because he didn't seem bothered. Maybe that was the French way – they just let it all hang out and shrugged *'c'est la vie'* in a sexy manner. He pressed on, moving his way around my inner thighs and the nascent pubic hair that was attempting to grow there on the red raw skin. I tried not to squirm. After what felt like an eternity, he threw the towel back over me and made his pronouncement.

'I think you 'ave pulled your abductor,' he said, with a flourish. 'I am going to give you some exercises to do, and try an ultrasound.'

'An ultrasound?' I said. 'Do you think there's something in there? Like . . . an alien?'

Frenchie the physio chuckled. 'No, no, we do ze ultrasound on ze affected areas because it reduces ze 'ealing time of soft tissue injuries. You see?'

I nodded, even though I didn't. It made no sense to me that a process usually reserved for expectant mothers could somehow help my injured thigh. Five minutes later he was back down at my warzone, smothering ultrasound gel all over it. If I'd had any dignity, it had now officially departed.

'You need to rest for two weeks,' he announced when he was finished, as if this was the breeziest thing in the world, as if I had two weeks to just hang around on the sofa doing sweet fuck all. DID HE NOT KNOW I WAS DOING A MARATHON? HAD I NOT MENTIONED IT?

Eat, Drink, Run.

An icy feeling of dread swept through my body. This was terrible. It was worse than terrible. It was like the time I got dumped in Nando's multiplied by the morning I came round from a three-day cocaine bender in a stranger's flat times infinity. I caught myself then, tried to see a positive. I was not panicking because I had been dumped by a weed-smoking loser who I had mistaken for the love of my life. I was not panicking because I couldn't remember seventy-two hours of my life. I was panicking because I couldn't exercise for two weeks. If younger Bryony could see this version of Bryony, she wouldn't recognise herself. It was a definite improvement on the whole Nando's/drug bender thing.

But still.

'Rest for two weeks? I couldn't possibly!' I was due to run a half marathon in three weeks. If I did nothing for a fortnight I was going to be seriously behind on my training. I would almost inevitably lose all the fitness I had worked so hard for and BE RIGHT BACK AT THE BEGINNING, A FAT, HUFFING, PUFFING SLUG WHO COULDN'T GET ROUND THE COMMON. Frenchie the physio shrugged at this, as if I was being overdramatic or something. Moi? He was clearly happy to be paid £85 to molest the peculiar thighs of strange women if they insisted on ignoring all professional advice and destroying their bodies. He was obviously one of those perverts that I had read

180

about in old weekly magazines you found at the dentist. Or at the physio, now I came to think of it.

'You do not rest, you do not do the marathon,' he said, bluntly, and so once again, that was that.

Who would have thought all those months ago that the hardest bit of marathon training was going to be rest? Back in May, when I had accidentally talked myself into this whole jolly enterprise, I thought that the most impossible thing was going to be motivating myself to get off the sofa. But now here I was essentially imprisoned by it, and all I wanted to do was get off it and jig up and down on the spot. I wanted to run up and down the one flight of stairs we co-owned with the bank. I wanted to do a yoga class, or a Pilates class, or *anything* active, really.

One night I had a dream that I was running the marathon – no, that I was flying through it, almost. But then, at mile eleven, I tripped and fell. I lay sprawled on the pavement as other runners sped past me, oblivious to the pain I was in. Eventually some strange creatures appeared: human, but only just. They had purple eyes and three pairs of arms. They told me they were going to help me, that I had broken my leg and they would repair me. I refused to listen – it was just a small fall, a slight graze, no more than the one I had sustained drunkenly that night in the Cotswolds. But they were adamant. They stretchered me away to

181

what looked like a cross between an ambulance and a space ship, me screaming the whole time but nobody apparently hearing. The spectators on the side of the road were cheering on the other runners; Harry and Edie couldn't see me even though I waved frantically at them. Once inside the strange vehicle, we started to fly away. Below I could see all the other runners, crossing the finish line, a feat that got further and further away as we soared into the clouds and then space. I woke sitting bolt upright in bed, cold sweat pooling between every bit of fat on me – my boobs, my bum, my red raw thighs. 'I had a terrible nightmare!' I almost screamed, and then Harry had to spend an hour stroking my back until I fell asleep. It was bizarre how the marathon was now taking over not just every waking moment of my life, but every non-waking moment too.

Eventually I dispatched Harry to Holland and Barrett to buy a curious selection of things that Dr Google told me would make me better – even though, deep down, I knew that the only thing that was going to make me better was staying exactly where I was, motionless on the sofa. L-Glutamine powder, which apparently helps to build muscles. A selection of supplements that would help my joints. Fish oil, because fish oil helps everything, right? Epsom salts, which apparently help muscle pain. Magnesium spray, which is said to bring down inflammation. Harry returned weighed down with bags, looking like a sort of fitness Father Christmas. 'From now on, we are only eating lentils, vegetables and lean, white meat!' I exclaimed, having spent another hour or so perusing the wisdom of Dr Google.

'Lentils make you fart,' said Harry.

'If farting is what it is going to take to get me up and out of the house, then I am afraid to say that I will be farting for the forseeable!'

I drink the L-Glutamine dissolved in water, down the supplements, gag at the fish oil. I run a bath, and examine the tub of Epsom salts. It advises users to gradually build up the amounts you add to the water, as 'some rare side effects including irregular heartbeat, nausea and dizziness have been known to occur'. I empty the contents into the bath, once more casting aside the wisdom of experts. I get in for a long soak. It feels just like a normal bath – until half an hour after I get out of it, when my bowels send me barrelling to the loo. Oh well, if flatulence is what it takes, then flatulence it is.

In the morning I spray the magnesium on my thigh. It produces a strange, tingling sensation, not too dissimilar from burning. But it's a better pain than the throbbing of my injured abductor, so I apply more. Suddenly, I feel my lady parts burning. Oh God, I've put too much on. 'MAGNESIUM MUFF,' I scream to Harry. 'MAGNESIUM MUFF!'

Eat, Drink, Run.

'Do I need my nurse's kit again?' asks Edie, as Harry wipes away tears of laughter.

About a week into my convalescence, I am flicking idly through Twitter when I notice a tweet by a journalist I know. 'Out of order for Private Eye to mock @bryony_gordon who writes about running to help manage mental illness and is training for a marathon.' Below is a photo she has taken of the 'humorous' article they have included in their latest issue.

'THE AMAZING PHILIPPA PAGE NEW YEAR "GET FIT 'N' LEAN" DETOX DIET WORKOUT' is the headline. 'The *Eye*'s top columnist, Philippa Page, has undergone a total transformation in just two weeks, as she submits herself to a gruelling regime of strenuous, hard-core Belgian Navy exercises and rigorous low-carb, high-gluten microbiotic diet of twice daily soya milk, kale and nut smoothies. And, as you can see, the results are incredible!'

Below are three pictures of three columnists in workout gear – before, one week later, and after. The first, 'before', is a slim woman who works for the *Sunday Times*, the second, 'one week later', a marginally larger *Observer* columnist, and the third, 'after', an unflattering picture of me running to work, looking rather fat, to accompany a piece I had written in the *Telegraph*. 'You too can reboot your life, take back control of your body and fill up pages and pages of otherwise empty space, as editors search desperately for something to print in January.'

Private Eye is a satirical magazine that sends up people who work in journalism and politics, and I'm used to appearing in its pages – I've been Bryony Gormless, and featured in its 'Street of Shame' column for my appalling behaviour in my twenties. Most of these I have laughed off. I like to think I have a sense of humour about it – furthermore, it is seen as something of an honour, no matter how dubious, to be viewed as worthy of inclusion in its pages. But I don't find this funny. How dare they take the piss out of a fat bird who is trying her hardest to do something good? What right do they have? What does it matter that I look huge in the picture, my running backpack unflatteringly making every bump and lump of my body obvious, not to mention the Lycra leggings I am in? Should I not be able to write about running if I am not eight stone and svelte, with a figure like Karlie Kloss? I'm sure that as they sat in the office, the people who put the piss-taking item together thought it was hilarious that the *Telegraph* was trying to pass me off as some vision of health. But they weren't, actually. They were, for once, a newspaper showing that overweight people, imperfect people, can do exercise too. It just so happened to be January, when the glut of 'new year, new you' articles take hold. But this wasn't a 'new year, new you' article. It was simply a piece

185

about old me trying to get fit at new year. I thanked the journalist who had tweeted the piece for bringing it to my attention, and sat stewing for several hours on the sofa.

For me, signing up to do the marathon was partly about raising funds for a mental health charity, and showing the effect running can have on depression. But it was also to try and prove that someone like me could do it: it was about standing up for anyone who has ever felt crap comparing themselves to the images of perfection we are so frequently shown in magazines and on television. Now all I could think about were the folds of fat on my stomach, the folds of fat that were inevitably getting larger as I sat stationary on the sofa waiting for my abductors to get better. The truth was, my body – the body that *Private Eye* had mocked for not looking 'fit 'n' lean' – had actually enabled me to run eleven miles on several occasions. It had taken me to Tower Bridge, helped me climb up a hill in Ibiza. Man, even before all of this it had given birth to a baby. It was the right body, because it was mine. But as I sat on the sofa I could only see it as the wrong body. It wasn't moving anywhere, it hurt, and now, to top it all off, it was being mocked on the pages of a magazine.

I thought back to a run I had done just before I got injured, a quick scoot along the banks of the Thames that I had managed in a lunch break. As I was running back I passed a pub, outside of which a group of men shivered as they smoked fags and drank their pints. 'LOOK AT THE TITS ON YOU!' one of them bellowed as I bounced past. I felt full of burning shame, but used it to power myself past them that much faster. Now it felt like the whole world was laughing at my tits. I felt miserable, defeated.

'We're going to the pub,' I said to Harry when I phoned him. 'Let's book a babysitter.'

'Are you sure that's a good idea?' he replied. It was a Monday, not natural pub time, and a night on the alcohol and fags wasn't exactly what the physio had ordered. But fuck the physio, I thought. Perhaps what I really needed was to let rip a little. To relax. 'I think it's the best idea I've had in a long time,' I said.

It is freezing cold, but I don't care: I want to sit outside and chain-smoke as I drink. I want to down beers back to back and puff on fags endlessly. If I'm going to do this, then I'm going to do it properly. Go big or go home, as they say. And I don't much fancy going home, given that I have spent the last couple of weeks there resting on the sofa watching repeats of *Frasier*.

'This is to celebrate my leg getting better,' I say, raising my pint glass to Harry's. I don't actually know if my leg *is* better, but it has been almost two weeks and I am due my check-up with Frenchie the Physio the next morning, who will surely congratulate me for taking his advice and resting, for being an exemplary patient. Maybe he will even notice that in my boredom I've Immaced my bikini line, that the chafing seems to have gone down because I haven't been rubbing my fat thighs together while running. In this post-pre-marathon world, anything is possible.

I drink the pint pretty quickly even for me – ten minutes, twelve max. 'Slow down there, sweetheart!' urges Harry, who is halfway through his, but I don't intend to do anything slowly tonight. I've had enough of being slow. I want to speed up, to get going, to be back out there. I walk to the bar. My leg feels fine. Another pint please, sir. Four down and I am feeling on top of the world. It isn't even 9 p.m. on Monday. Just imagine what the rest of the week might bring?

Outside in the beer garden, Harry and I are completely alone. They have turned the heaters on for us, but even that hasn't coaxed any of the pub regulars out. They huddle around the fire inside and look at us as if we are mad people. Who cares? We are. Or at least I am – Harry is just mad by association. 'I'm really proud of you,' he says, and that's how I know he's drunk. Harry hasn't done sober emotion since 1983, when his parents took his Optimus Prime away. 'I'm really, really proud of you,' he repeats.

I smile. 'Do you know something?' I don't give him a chance to reply. '*I'm* really proud of me too. I've never done anything proud-making, and now I'm

going to run a bloody marathon. Did I mention that?'
It's quite possible I am drunk too. 'I never thought
I'd see the day when I felt desperate to go for a run,'
I say, drawing deep on a Marlboro Light, 'but here
we are!' I raise my glass, down its contents. 'Here's
to . . . ME!' Then I fall over on the way to the bar,
and the next thing I know I am at home, with my
head down the loo.

The good news is, I don't seem to have done any
further damage to my leg. When I wake up I am able
to walk without the slightest twinge, and I feel confident that Frenchie the Physio will pass me to run.
The bad news is . . . well, I'm not feeling so well. My
head is thumping, my throat is sore, and I have a
hacking cough. But I am putting it down to a hangover
– that and the fact I was sick last night. Of course
I'd feel a bit dodgy after knocking back that much
beer. I expect that once I am up and out there, I will
start to feel better.

'Gosh,' I say to Harry, 'my tolerance of booze has
gone down a bit since I started training for the
marathon!'

He looks at me sternly. 'Bryony, you drank six pints
and smoked a packet and a half of fags.'

Whatever. You've got to live a little. I walk to
Frenchie the Physio's surgery and notice how the cold
air hits my chest, even through my giant, padded,

winter jacket. My throat makes a sort of strangulated sound every time I breathe in, like a Victorian death rattle. My body is just clearing itself out from the previous night's excesses, I tell myself. Before long I will be feeling right as rain. Right on cue, it starts to pour down – the kind of icy rain that would be snow if it wasn't so damn cold. I make a run for the physio's, but have to stop to cough up what appears to be part of a lung. Better out than in, I suppose!

In the physio waiting room, I am grateful for the heating. Even the skeleton looks a little cheerier in this warmth. Frenchie takes me to his room and asks me how I am. 'Great!' I try to say, but it comes out as a series of coughs and splutters. Never mind – it wasn't as if communication was our strong point anyway. I start to take off my trainers and remove my jeans. Frenchie looks alarmed – I don't know why, given that just the other week he was having a good grope round the outer edges of my lady garden. How come he's suddenly got all coy? 'I geev you preevacy,' he says, disappearing out of the room. I climb on to the bed and anxiously await his return. Lying down, I start to cough again, so hard that he races back in with a box of tissues and a glass of water. 'You OK?'

'Splutter, hack, cough,' I reply. He nods and starts to feel around my abductors. 'I do ze ultrasound again, and zen I tape you.'

'You what?'

'I put tape on ze thighs and ze knees. The tape, eet ees magic. Eet eemproves ze blood flow to ze muscles. Eet 'elp you when you run.'

'I can run again?'

'Yes! Your abductor, eet ees much better,' he nods. I attempt a sigh of relief, but instead I seem to bark like a seal. 'But you might want to go to a doctor about ze coughing.'

I walk to work covered in running tape, looking like a woman marked for plastic surgery. I can run again! So why do I feel so low? At the office, Joe and Eleanor tell me to stay away from them. 'You've got the plague,' they say. My boss tells me to go and see the work doctor. 'You look really sick, Bryony,' she says, 'and you don't want to take a chance now that you're training for a marathon. I know you don't like to make a big deal out of it,' she says sarcastically, 'but I'm asking you to look after yourself.'

I book an appointment with the office GP, just to get them off my back. No doubt he will tell me I have some sort of twenty-four-hour fever that will burn off with a good night's sleep. Hoarse, wheezing and feeling ever so slightly woozy, I climb the stairs to his office. 'Good grief,' he says, as I fall through the door. 'You do not look good!'

'I don't feel great,' I nod, and then I gratefully flop into a chair.

Eat, Drink, Run.

More probing, more prodding, this time with a stethoscope and one of those wooden sticks that they usually have to use on toddlers to get them to keep their mouths open during an oral examination. Lights are shone in my throat and my ear. I just want to go home, and sleep until the morning. 'Well,' announces the doctor, 'the good news is I don't *think* it's pneumonia. But it's definitely bronchitis. I'm going to write you a prescription for some antibiotics, and put you on bed rest for a week. I've been reading your marathon updates, but for the next ten days or so, NO RUNNING!'

God damn.

The date that I should be running a half marathon, according to my training schedule, comes and goes without me moving a muscle below my chest. I am confined to my bed, covered in Vicks VapoRub. I console myself with the fact it is not my daughter's nappy cream. To keep myself busy, I set about organising the Mental Health Mates first anniversary walk, which is coming up that weekend. I order huge balloons, and ten boxes of brownies, and will myself better for it. If I send positive vibes out to the world, surely the world will send them back to me.

Three days into this particular period of inactivity, I receive an email from a man named Tim. Tim is a personal trainer who has worked with various magazine editors and celebrities to get them fit for big endurance tests

– swims across Lake Geneva and, yes, marathons. He has heard from a mutual friend that I have had a few setbacks in my training, and wonders if he could offer some help. He has a couple of places for the half marathon in Paris in two weeks time, and would be more than happy to go round it with me. Did I want to meet for a coffee? I dialled the number at the end of his email before he had a chance to reconsider his extremely generous offer.

Two days later, feeling marginally better, I meet Tim for a lemon and ginger tea. Tim has run umpteen marathons, and has a place for London as well. He tells me not to worry that I haven't been able to stick to the training plan. 'Say I came and asked you to produce a guide for everyone on how to get over mental illness,' he says. 'You'd tell me to bugger off. There isn't a one-size-fits-all approach for marathons. I had to train one man who was so large that we had to do all the preparation in the swimming pool. Marathon day was the first day he'd actually run, and he did it in six hours. We follow your body. We can get you to that start line, I promise.' He has followed my story with interest, likes what I am doing, and would like to offer me coaching for free.

'If you want,' he continues, 'I can even get you to the finish line.' I let out an audible gasp. 'I can run round the whole thing with you for support. I have a place, but I've done a load of marathons so I'd love to use it to help you.'

Eat, Drink, Run.

I am speechless and totally overwhelmed by the generosity of his offer. Here is someone who will literally hold my hand as I finish my training – and not just that, but take on the day itself. I throw my arms around him. 'You can be my marathon carer?!' I eventually manage to mumble. 'I would love that!'

As I leave the café, my phone rings. It is Jason, at Kensington Palace. 'I just wanted to let you know that His Royal Highness has considered your offer and would love to do the interview with you.' On a cold street, I begin to weep.

That numinous thing is making itself known again. I can feel it everywhere – in the air I breathe, the water I drink and the food I eat. That Sunday, I get up for the Mental Health Mates anniversary walk, and realise I am feeling so much better. Before I leave, I check the inbox to see how many registrations we have – over seventy. It blows my mind that we have grown so much in just a year. There is an email from a girl apologising, but she doesn't think she will be able to make it. She is feeling too low, too depressed. I type out a reply. 'I totally understand and have been there before, but just in case you change your mind and want a cuddle, here's my number.' Then I put on my sports bra, leggings and trainers – I'm feeling in such a good mood that I might even attempt a run after the walk.

In Hyde Park, at the same place I had so nervously

gone to a year before, not knowing if anyone would turn up, I start to blow up balloons. Harry and Edie are salivating over the brownies we have been donated. I check my phone to see a flurry of messages on our Mental Health Mates Whatsapp group, people excitedly letting one another know that they are on their way. Then I see a text from a number I don't recognise. 'Hello Bryony,' it reads. 'You very kindly replied to my email about feeling too depressed to come to the walk. Well, I'm seeing your message as a sign. I think I might come for that hug. Jen x'

I feel a bit tingly inside. People start to arrive. Even some of the staff at Heads Together have come to tweet the walk out on their social media. I feel inordinately proud of what we have all achieved, and get a little tearful as I address everyone before we head off for the walk. Jen introduces herself. I notice that she is also dressed top to toe in running gear. 'I thought, well if I'm going out, I might as well go for a run after,' she smiles. 'Get the endorphins properly pumping. I love running, but just haven't felt well enough for it recently. Your message has given me the motivation I needed.'

I look at Jen with tears in my eyes. 'Can I come for a run with you? I don't know if I mentioned, but I've got this marathon coming up, and I haven't been so well either recently. I could really do with a bit of a jog . . .' She smiles at me. It is done.

And so it is that after the anniversary walk, I find myself gently plodding around central London with a woman I didn't know that morning – a woman who also has OCD and depression. Ten miles later, as Jen and I settle down for a post-run burger and check out all the pictures people have posted from the walk, I realise there really is magic in the world. There is magic everywhere.

8

To Paris

And there is nothing more magic than Paris in the spring, or so the song goes.

In a ridiculously good mood, I ask my mum if she'd be OK looking after Edie for the weekend, and book Eurostar tickets so that Harry can come with me to Paris for the half marathon. 'It will be so romantic!' I say, fluttering my eyelashes and heaving my bosom at him. 'We can feed each other oysters and drink red wine and—'

'And you can run thirteen miles. *Très romantique.*'

'Just think of the nice walks by the Seine. Or the time we can spend in our hotel room.' I raise my eyebrows in what I hope to be a seductive manner. Perhaps Paris will give me the impetus to have sex with my husband.

'You booked the Holiday Inn next to the station,' points out Harry.

Eat, Drink, Run.

'It has three stars!' I am trying to be enthusiastic. 'And anyway, who cares that it's not the Ritz. All that matters is that we will get some time alone . . .'

'Technically, we're not going to get any time alone. Technically, we are going with your trainer. I've probably had more romantic weekends by myself in my childhood bedroom.'

'There's no need to be so moody about it. Just think of the trees in blossom, the charm of spring . . . what's that Sinatra song?'

'It's called "April in Paris". We'll be going the first weekend of March,' he says, being the sexy pedant that I fell in love with way back when. 'Also, it says it's going to rain all weekend. But otherwise, sure. Let's blow all our savings and go to Paris so I can stand in the freezing cold getting soaking wet as you do a half marathon with some strange man you don't even know.'

'I've had a coffee with him! He trains famous people! He's like this rugged, chiselled athlete who is married to a gorgeous doctor! He's hardly going to be interested in me!'

'It's not that I don't trust you implicitly, Bryony, but he's basically the only reason I'm hitching a ride on this so-called "romantic weekend"' – he even does the quote marks with his fingers – 'and I know how gullible you can be. Remember when that man came knocking on the door saying he was selling cleaning products for charity, and you went upstairs to the bedroom to get your wallet, only to return and find that he had disappeared – with Edie's scooter?'

'That was different.'

'We were lucky he hadn't taken Edie too.'

'All right, that was foolish.'

'The point is, how do you even know he's going to turn up for the half marathon? How do you even know there IS a half marathon?'

'Because I've Googled it. The Semi de Paris. Over 200,000 people take part in it every year. It's one of the biggest in the world.'

'All the better for him to trample over your exhausted body at mile twelve without anybody seeing. Were your safety not my primary concern, you'd be *toute seule, ma cherie.*'

'You're saying that you're basically coming as my carer?'

'That's exactly what I am saying. And that's exactly what I am. Husbands occasionally get treated by their wives . . . and not like slaves.'

I start to pack. Who am I fooling? I'm not going to Paris for a romantic weekend that happens to include some exercise. I'm basically being escorted there by my two carers so that I can fulfil my dream of running a half marathon.

Mon dieu. I've changed.

On the Eurostar, I begin to wonder if I'm not actu-ally gatecrashing a romantic weekend between Harry

199

and Tim. Any doubts that carer number one might have had about carer number two disappear before we have even entered the Channel Tunnel. They get on like the proverbial house on fire, with Harry so impressed by Tim's athletic skills that he gets a special look about his face, a look I last saw when we were 'courting' back in 2011. The sense of bromance is so strong that Harry starts to puff out his chest every time Tim talks; I swear my husband's voice actually gets deeper when he tells Tim about how he was a champion rower at school. I had no idea my husband had such abilities in a coxless four; it must have slipped his mind when he was recounting his school years to me, which at the time mostly seemed to include drinking and smoking round the back of the bike sheds with his mates. Still, who am I to doubt the athletic prowess of my husband? Even if I wanted to, I wouldn't be able to get a word in edgeways given the amount these two are roaring like lions.

Once in Paris, I fancy that we might have a lunch of steak tartare, frites and red wine, but Tim is having none of it. 'Eating raw meat from a restaurant you're not used to the day before a half marathon?' he says in complete disbelief, as if I have just suggested we go for a swim in the Seine or attempt to break into the Élysée Palace. 'Are you mad?'

'You know I'm mad,' is my answer. 'Mad is what I

do. If I were sane, I would not be about to do a half marathon.'

'Actually,' interjects Harry, 'I've not seen you so calm and rational since you started training. All this getting up early to go for runs, followed by breakfasts of porridge: it's almost as if you're trying to be a normal person.'

'OK,' I smirk. 'Well, let's be normal people and go and look at some art galleries, see some sights. I've heard the Musée d'Orsay is lovely at this time of year.'

'You should totally do that,' says Harry sheepishly. 'But me and Tim were thinking of trying to find somewhere we could watch the game?'

'The game,' I repeat.

'Yeah, Man United are going to slay Bournemouth,' says Tim.

I glare at my husband. 'Well, Harry's a huge Manchester United fan, aren't you, darling? Never stops banging on about Eric Cantona and Alex Ferguson. What's your favourite chant again?'

'Tim doesn't want to hear me sing,' he snaps.

'Go on, mate!' urges Tim.

'Well, I'll be leaving you boys to it. See you later!' And off I strop, to see if there's somewhere I can stuff my face with cake. Nice, safe, cake.

In a café somewhere in the depths of Paris, I stuff my face with chocolate gateau and realise the enormity of what I am about to do. I can't even think about the Prince Harry interview, which is only a couple of weeks off, and what I am going to ask him: right now, all that I can contemplate is the 13.1 miles ahead of me. Thirteen point one. That's a long way. That's quite a distance. It's the kind of distance you should probably do by car, or bus, or at the very least on a bicycle. But here I am in a city I don't know with a trainer I don't know getting ready to do it by *foot*. And what is even more daunting is that it's only half the distance I am going to have to do in just under two months' time. I have made a terrible mistake, a huge error. I want to take it all back, tell everyone that I was experiencing delusions of grandeur but that I have now realised that I am just a fat girl with a huge pair of knockers and there's no way I can do a mara—

PING!

My phone starts flashing, with Whatsapp messages from the Mental Health Mates. 'Thinking of you, Bry!' 'You can do this!' 'You're totally awesome, remember that!' Cheered, I look at my email and discover several notifications telling me that I have been sponsored for the marathon. The total now stands at almost £16,000, which is incredible given that a few months ago I had barely allowed myself to believe that I could raise £10,000.

I decide to go for a walk. I'm in Paris, and I might as well have a good look around it even if my husband would rather spend his time here in a bar watching a sport he doesn't like with a man he barely knows. I walk along the river, go to the Musée d'Orsay, remind myself how lucky I am to be on this journey – even if that does sound almost unbearably cheesy. I like cheesy. I think cheesy is good – it's certainly an improvement on my twenties, when I was a cynical old misery guts who thought the world was out to get her. Breathing in the Parisian air, I remember that the world isn't actually that interested in me. The world is too busy facing its own struggles, fighting its own battles. All I can do is get on with fighting my own the best I know how. All I can do is try and let others know that if I can do it, then they can too.

Once Harry has finished playing at having a clue about football, Tim and I set off to pick up our race packs from the vast town of tents that have been erected next to the start line – also known as the 'race village'. Harry would be coming too, if he hadn't drunk his bodyweight in Kronenbourg during 'the game' and announced that he needed a lie down. 'He got a bit carried away,' says Tim, as Harry staggers off into the distance. 'Sorry about that.'

'Don't apologise. It's good to finally be getting some time alone with you.' Tim looks a little terrified. 'I mean, you know, to talk running.' Tim remains silent.

'Nothing else.' I note the uncomfortable, rictus grin that spreads across his face. 'I'm not trying it on with you, if that's what you're worried about.'

'I wasn't, Bryony. I was just waiting for you to stop talking. Do you ever go quiet?'

'Apart from when I'm on a Eurostar with two men talking sport? No, not really. I'm not fond of quiet. Gives me too much time to, you know' – I twirl my finger next to my head – 'think!'

'How have you found training alone then?'

'Well, mostly I've ended up having fantasies that involve Poldark, going to the Tokyo Olympics, and becoming best friends with Jennifer Lawrence,' I confess.

'Right,' says Tim. 'Most people just listen to music. But now you've got me to talk to. And I'm looking forward to it. But first things first: tomorrow is your first competitive race, right?'

'Right,' I nod, slightly concerned that he thinks I am hoping for a podium finish. Frankly, I will be glad just to finish, full stop.

'And it will also be your last before the big day. Which, incidentally, is in just under two months' time.'

Does he think I don't have the date etched on my brain? That I haven't been chalking it off every morning as if I were a prisoner waiting to finish a life sentence?

'So tomorrow is the dress rehearsal. Tomorrow, aside from the distance we are going to run, we treat it like marathon day. We get up and eat the same breakfast.

We wear the same trainers, smother on the same amount of Vaseline.'

'Of course,' I say, seriously. Vaseline, I realise, is serving an increasingly important role in my life, one I could not have previously imagined.

'And most of all, we enjoy it.'

'Yes!' I beam, motivated by his little speech. We pick up our race numbers, go back to our three-star hotel, and I try to sleep. As Harry snores out his beer breath next to me, it comes to me surprisingly easily – a sweet, dreamless sleep, the type you get when you realise you are finally safe. For the first time in my life, I feel like I am being carried: by Tim, by the Mental Health Mates, by all the kind people who are sponsoring me in this crazy endeavour. And that, I realise, is worth signing up to do a marathon in itself.

The alarm goes off and for a moment all is well. I feel refreshed, ready, raring to go – and so I should after almost twelve hours' sleep. Then I pull open the curtains and see that Paris is in the midst of a storm. A raging, whirling, rainstorm. The sky is slate grey and the wind is battering branches of trees backwards and forwards. Harry assesses his iPhone app. 'Oof, doesn't look good,' he says, groggily. 'There's a 100 per cent chance of rain ALL DAY. Would you mind if I stayed in bed?'

But I can deal with rain. I've dealt with OCD and depression. I've dealt with alopecia and bulimia. I've dealt with terrible relationships. I've dealt with a raging cocaine habit. A little bit of rain is not going to ruin my day. In fact, it might even improve it – stop me from getting too warm as I run. 'It'll cool me down!' I say, trying to muster as much enthusiasm as possible. 'It will be like a light Caribbean rain shower on my skin the whole way round the course! Lovely!'

Outside, a branch crashes to the pavement.

Harry decides to stay in bed and I can't say I blame him. He promises that he will be there at the halfway point and finish line, but in the meantime he's just going to catch up on some more sleep. I thank the heavens – if not for the rain then for the £150 anorak I bought way back when. My ridiculously expensive tights also promise to keep out moisture – although looking at the downpour outside, I'm not entirely sure the manufacturers meant *this* kind of moisture.

After a breakfast of gooey porridge in the hotel restaurant, Tim and I set off on the Metro with thousands of other nervous-looking half marathon runners. Getting off at our stop, somewhere on the outskirts of Paris, we trudge through thick mud to the race village. For the first time I look at the route. 'It's not very exciting,' says Tim. 'You basically run through all the industrial areas and just as you're reaching the nice bits like Notre Dame, you turn back.'

What had I expected it to be? A chic and glamorous half marathon decked out in Chanel? It was taking place at the end of Paris Fashion Week, but that was where the glamour ended. Today, Paris looked like it had been swallowed by clouds; today, Paris appeared to have been washed away in a terrible flood. I was going to have to get down and dirty. I was going to have to get wet. 'Here, take this,' Tim says, handing me some extra 'waterproofs'. All the sweat-wicking clothes in the world are, it seems, no match for the bin bags that the worried-looking race organisers are now handing out.

'Is it going to be like this at the London Marathon?' I ask Tim, as we tear holes for our heads in our rubbish bags.

'If anything, it will be the opposite,' says Tim, nonchalantly. 'Usually it gets too hot at the end of April, and then you have people passing out with heat stroke.'

'Oh,' I say, quietly. I don't know what is worse: the thought of having to swim a half marathon or run a full one in baking heat.

Tim and I trudge through yet more mud towards the start line. It's like being at Glastonbury, except without the prospect of any alcohol or mind-altering drugs. Gosh, what I would do for mind-altering drugs right now. They might make what I'm about to do a little bearable. But I need to stay positive. Craving illegal drugs is not the kind of thing a professional athlete does when they are on the start line of a big race – though given all those reports about doping at the Olympics, maybe it is. Still, it's unlikely that they're craving an Ecstasy pill, or that anyone is going to hand me one. Oh God, the pressure is turning me into a junkie. I need to pull myself together. I need to focus.

I try and draw on the energy of the thousands of runners around me. I remind myself that we are all in the same boat. Or we wish we were in a boat, given how much it is chucking it down. 'The last time I saw rain and wind like this was during a cyclone on my honeymoon in Mauritius,' shouts Tim, above the din of the weather. 'At least then we didn't have to run a half marathon and could stay sheltered drinking cocktails in the bar!'

'That's good to know,' I lie. 'Good to know.'

Mmmm, cocktails.

'Is it normal that right now all I want to do is take drugs?' I say.

'WHAT'S THAT?' shouts Tim.

'I SAID, IS IT NORMAL THAT RIGHT NOW ALL I WANT TO DO IS TAKE DRUGS?' Tim shrugs to say he can't hear me. Sadly the same cannot be said of the woman on my other side, who seems horrified by what I have just admitted. And there I was thinking that the language barrier would protect me.

Never mind – I have more important things to worry about. Like keeping warm. Christ, it is cold – if I didn't have this rubbish bag on, everyone would be able to see just how cold by the alertness of my nipples. At least being dressed as a kitchen bin has its benefits. I jog up and down on the spot, and am grateful when the crowd starts to move towards the start line – something I never thought I would feel. Suddenly, we're across it! I am officially running my first competitive race – though what with all the crowds of people around me, I feel more like I am shuffling through it. Indeed, for the first two kilometres it is almost impossible to get going properly, such is the volume of the crowd. I decide that this is a blessing in disguise. At least I can conserve some energy.

As the crowd starts to thin out I become a little over-excited. I break into what can only be described as a sprint – or at least my version of one. 'SLOW DOWN!' shouts Tim, and for a second I allow myself to smugly believe that I am going too fast for him. But no. As he catches up to me I can see he has barely broken a sweat – in fact, I can see that he is *walking*. 'You don't want to go out too quickly,' he cautions. 'If you do that, you're in danger of burning out too soon. Go as slowly as you can.'

'But if I do that, you'll basically have to start crawling in order not to overtake me.' I am in some distress at how my version of fast seems to be his version of . . . well, almost remaining stationary.

'Don't worry about me,' he says. 'Remember, I'm only here to get you round.'

Eat, Drink, Run.

I go down a gear and settle into a light jog. It feels good. Even the rain seems to have stopped. At five kilometres I gratefully take one of the bananas being handed out by volunteers, then spend the next 100 metres trying not to slip on the skins that have been discarded by other runners. 'The French,' shrugs Tim. 'They like to make things difficult for themselves.'

But not too difficult . . . it occurs to me that I have seen only a handful of spectators so far on the course, and even they might have been rubbish pickers. Clearly the general public have decided that if we want to spend the morning outside in weather conditions last seen in the Old Testament, then they will respect our decision – but they're buggered if they're going to stand outside and applaud us for it. Still, I don't care about people I don't know lining the streets. I am just looking forward to seeing Harry. I imagine how proud he will be as I run past him, how I might even run towards him and give him a kiss. 'Better get my smiley face on for when we go past him at 10k!' I think to myself.

But at 10k the rain has started back up and my husband is nowhere to be seen. I tell myself that perhaps he has had to take shelter in a nearby café. After all, the wind is picking up to the point that it is able to turn the volunteers' umbrellas inside out.

Maybe it's the downturn in the weather – who knew when we woke up that it could actually get worse?

– or maybe it's the fact I haven't seen Harry. But by 12k, my spirits seriously start to flag. No matter how much I run, I cannot seem to get warm. The damp seems to have seeped through my bin bag and my £150 anorak, and I can feel the chafing between my sports bra and my boobs. Wincing, I try to ignore it. It's as if my body is listening. Suddenly, I am overcome by an overwhelming urge to do a number two. 'I need the loo!' I wail to Tim.

'Can it wait until the end?' he says breezily, as if my bowels weren't about to explode. Oh God, was my overriding memory of marathon training milestones going to be poo-related? 'It's just they're not that generous on the portable loos here. Just seven or so kilometres to go!' He is so cheery, so relentlessly positive that I feel it might crush him to tell him the truth: I am scared I am going to shit myself again.

I decide to stop for a moment, and do some deep breathing. I will my bowels to behave. I start a light jog, and something amazing happens: it's as if the motion of the movement has shifted the shit back to a position where it doesn't want to come out. They don't tell you about *that* in running magazines. I feel euphoric for a kilometre or so, but then the chafing seems to get worse and this time I feel as if it might actually be drawing blood. My poor bosoms, the thing that Harry so loved about me, ruined by running. Let it be his punishment for not bothering to show up, I tell myself.

211

Eat, Drink, Run.

By now a gale force wind has begun to blow around the course. My cheeks sting with pain. I go to put up the anorak's hood in an attempt to keep the cold off my face, unaware that it has spent the last fifteen or so kilometres filling with rain. It empties over my head, and I think I might start to cry. Defeated, I stop running. 'I can't go on!' I wail to Tim, as I plod along the road. 'I CAN'T DO IT ANY MORE!'

'Bryony,' he says, fixing me with a stare as icy as the weather around us. 'When you're with me, we do NOT say can't. We only say can.'

Now where have I heard *that* before?

The only thing that gets me to the finish line is the thought of the steak tartare Tim has promised me I can have for lunch. I can taste it in my mouth, feel the raw mince on my tongue. Mmm, raw mince. I am practically salivating by the time I get to the end, and who's going to notice a bit of dribble given that the rest of me is already soaked to the skin with snot and rain?

As we cross the finish line, I come to an abrupt halt. I am exhausted. I am done. A thought flashes through my mind: in seven weeks, I am going to have to run that, and then do it *again*. I start to cry. 'What's wrong?' says Tim, as volunteers place our medals over our bin bag-covered necks. I am inconsolable. I feel as if I have just been told that my entire family has been wiped out by an asteroid. 'I'll tell you what's wrong,' I just about manage to splutter. 'It's that if you told me right now that I had to run another thirteen miles, I would use what energy I have left to STAMP ON YOUR HEAD.'

Back at the hotel, we meet Harry, who it turns out hasn't actually managed to get out of bed. I blink at him in soggy disbelief. 'You've been lying here all morning while I've been out doing a half marathon?'

'Well, if I'd known it was going to take you so long I totally would have come, but I thought you'd be round it in no time what with Tim accompanying you. Did you know that he did his quickest marathon in two and a half hours?!'

'I didn't,' I say, mentally calculating that it just took us twenty-three minutes longer to do a *half*. At this rate, I might actually end up being beaten by that dude who walked round the London course in a diving suit (it took him just under a week). There will be tortoises that have done marathons faster than me. There will be . . . slugs.

Goddamn those black slugs.

'I've run you a bath,' says Harry, nodding towards the luxurious avocado-green tub of our three-star hotel room. When I look in I realise it's the left-over water from the hour and a half soak he's just *endured*. But I don't care. I collapse into it, survey my exhausted body. It is indeed bleeding. Just below my chest are two saggy breast-shaped scars from where my boobs have rubbed against my skin, breaking it open. 'What do you think of my battle wounds?' I say, flashing my tits proudly at Harry as I re-emerge from the bathroom.

'Oh my GOD,' he screams. 'It's like you've been in a terrible accident. If I'd known this might happen when you signed up to do the marathon, I'd never have let you!'

'Rub Vaseline into me please,' I beg him, in what I hope is a seductive manner, and there, in our hotel room, we rewrite the very definition of a romantic weekend in Paris.

But I've done the half marathon, and I even have a bright, shiny medal to prove it. Once Harry has finished lathering petroleum jelly round my sore bits, we head out with Tim for steak tartare, and when I get up to use the loo, I realise that my legs appear to be stuck in the sitting position. They creak as I attempt to get down the stairs. But any pain I might feel is overtaken by a huge sense of pride. My body seems magical to me. I can't believe it just carried me through a half marathon.

'I have to say, I've never done a run in more miserable conditions,' laughs Tim. 'After that, you are going to find the London Marathon a walk in the park.'

On the Eurostar back, I drink a can of Kronenbourg and fall into a deep sleep. For the sake of my body and my sanity, I hope he is right.

*

Back in London, I decide that for once in my life, I am going to follow expert advice rather than haring off and believing I can do it my way. The experts, I have learnt at great cost to my health, really do know what they are talking about. The next weekend I drop down and do a casual twelve miles – to give my body a rest. 'Where's my wife and what have you done with her?' Harry demands to know when I tell him about my restful twelve-mile run. The weekend after that I head out and run a half marathon across London by myself, just for shits and giggles. That distance I once would only have contemplated by public transport is now a distance I can do alone. If the apocalypse was to come tomorrow, and I had to run multiple miles to go and rescue my family, I could. For the first time in my life I feel like a fully functioning and capable human being.

My self-belief is strong, and it feels unusual, but great. It doesn't even seem to matter that less charitable readers of the *Telegraph* keep taking it upon themselves to tell me that a cumbersome great lump like me shouldn't be doing a marathon. One morning, I get to work to find a thick envelope on my desk. I open it up and read the enclosed letter. 'Dear Bryony, I suggest you stop running including your run in the London Marathon, ESPECIALLY BECAUSE YOU ARE FAT. [He has written this in red ink, to make the point clearer.] I enclose photocopies of people who died running marathons. The only bodily contact sport which is usually healthy is SEX! [Again, he has written this word in red ink.] I am eighty and slim and have no pains. I walk to and from the shops, often carrying two heavy bags, at least 1.4 miles a day. Please mail me a reply.'

The last line is by far my favourite of the whole letter. What does he want? A *date*?

Whereas six months ago I would have ripped this kind of post up in fury, today I am just touched that someone has gone to all the effort of photocopying me old newspaper stories about people who have tragically died running marathons. And while I would be lying if I said that the physical enormity of what I have taken on didn't at some level terrify me, mostly the feeling I have about what I am doing is amazement. I am amazed when I look in the mirror and see glowing skin and clear eyes. I am amazed at the way my belly has shrunk, at the dresses I can slip myself into every morning – dresses I hadn't even dared to look at since before I got pregnant with Edie. But mostly, what amazes me is the complete absence of Jareth in my mind. Now I have got the obsessive-compulsive running in check and vowed only to follow Tim's advice, I feel as in control of my mental health as I ever have. This is such a strange sensation that I wake up every morning feeling almost reborn. I have such a spring in my step that I practically skip everywhere. The fundraising total continues to rise, along with my energy levels. I used to worry if I didn't have anything to worry about. But now I simply enjoy being; if something bad is going to happen, then it will happen, and there is no point wasting this positive time worrying about it.

We go away to my in-laws for a weekend. They live in the middle of nowhere in Wiltshire, and I imagine that the surrounding countryside will be a gorgeous place to do my next long run, which is fifteen whole miles. But on the morning I plan to do it, it is like Paris all over again. The rain pours down, the wind whips the trees. I feel anxious, defeated before I have even got going. Harry recognises the look on my face from the times I have been held prisoner by Jareth. 'Do not let your panic beat you,' he says, holding my hand, and he is right. I tie up my shoes, put that bloody £150 anorak back on, and set out to run.

Dodging branches through the woods, I realise I have the potential to get horribly lost – and in this rain, that's the last thing I need. I remember that the road near the house is about a mile into Salisbury, and decide to err on the side of caution. My God, this in itself is refreshing – give me the choice between safety and oblivion and usually I will choose the latter for fear of getting bored. And while the safe route may be boring, I figure that if boring doesn't involve getting lost in a storm and tearing my boob scars back open again, like some terrible, botched attempt at plastic surgery, then that's OK with me. This way I can pop into the house for loo breaks or a change of clothes if I need them. Goodness, listen to me: I sound like a mother or something!

I start running. And for the next three and a half hours, that's all I do – I run up that road, past the same old houses and the same old lampposts, and then I run back down it. Back and forth, back and forth I go, until I have done it sixteen times and my Fitbit tells me I have run fifteen miles. My legs feel empty but my heart feels full. I jump in the air, and then I notice that the rain has stopped, that the spring sun is shining down on me, that I am so warm that I need to take my anorak off.

I can't explain it, but I feel like some sort of super-hero. I may be exhausted, but I have never felt so alive. All those years feeling like a freak, all that time I thought that OCD controlled me. But I was wrong. I was so wrong. All along, I had the power. All along, I had this superpower that, if I tapped into it in the right way, could allow me to do incredible things. I squeal in delight, and I don't care who hears me. 'FUCK YOU, JARETH!' I woop. 'Fuck you and fuck OCD!' I jump up and down on the spot. I feel like a generator cranking out some mega wattage. I feel as if I am on full beam, as if I have been turned up to eleven. I am, I realise, a summerhouse that has spent most of its life boarded up, as if for a very long winter. The sockets may have been turned off, but the power has always been there untapped – dormant, waiting. Now I have worked out how to switch it on, and shrugged off all the scaffolding that has weighed me down for so long. And after all that time, I am beginning to feel truly tree.

9

To Kensington Palace

It never occurred to me that Prince Harry might be more nervous than I was about our interview. Like a small child who doesn't understand that the spider is just as scared of them as they are of it, I simply hadn't entertained the notion that the fifth in line to the throne might be experiencing some pre-interview jitters too.

In many ways, I was the lucky one. I had all the marathon training to take my mind off the fact that I was about to do the biggest interview of my career, and that had stopped me from thinking too much about all the ways I could balls it up. Sure, I'd allowed myself to think of a *few*. I could suddenly become flatulent – heaven knows that seemed to be the defining trait of the last few months. I could swear. I could call him Hazza. But mostly I felt that if I could run fifteen tedious miles up and down a road to Salisbury, I could do this. I realised, as I woke up on the morning of the interview, that the marathon training had instilled in me a confidence that no amount of alcohol, cocaine or therapy had managed before. It had given me some perspective, made me aware that the world was probably not going to end, that even if Armageddon had taken place in my head then outside everything was still spinning.

As I walked up the road to Kensington Palace, I had a moment of clarity. Whatever happened inside that historic building, it almost didn't matter. If Prince Harry said nothing of any interest, if I bored him to tears, then that was OK. My editor might be disappointed. I might not win any journalism awards. But in my head, I was already a winner. I had come this far, from a place that meant I often couldn't get out of bed because of depression, to the door of Kensington Palace. I had been the party columnist high on cocaine who wrote about her exploits, the one who felt hollow every time she pressed send on yet another vacuous piece of copy. Now I was going to interview a royal about his mental health. If it never got better than this, this being me standing at the entrance of a palace, then that was just fine by me

I had suggested we do the interview as a podcast, the idea being that this would make the young prince feel more relaxed than the prospect of a print interview in which his words could accidentally be taken out of context. I had got carried away with the idea: I loved the easy intimacy of podcasts, the fact that someone's voice could be there with you in your ear as you travelled to work on the tube, that you could be stuck in someone's armpit on the Northern line and yet inside Kensington Palace all at the same time.

Once we had got the green light, I had set about securing more people for the show. So far I had booked a nurse who had had a breakdown, a fourteen-year-old boy with OCD, and the writer Matt Haig, who wrote about his depression so brilliantly in *Reasons to Stay Alive*. I wanted to run the gamut from A to Z, from prince to, if not pauper, then normal person on the street. I wanted this podcast to show that all of human life was affected by mental illness, that it didn't matter who you were or what you did – it had the power to hit all of us at some point. Only by getting together and making that clear did we tilt the power balance in our favour – that was how we won the battle. And how better to do that than with a medium like the podcast, where anyone could listen anywhere, safe in the knowledge that not a single person could judge them.

And so *Mad World* was born. Prince Harry was to be the first guest – it wasn't as if I ever liked to do things by halves after all. On the morning of Wednesday, 22 March 2017, I wake up and select a beautiful summer dress I haven't fitted into since before the marathon training. It has tiny flowers printed on it, and seems just the right side of regal – the kind of thing 'one' might wear to Royal Ascot if one was fond of talking about themselves in the third person. It's a bit tight, but I can zip it up and that's all that matters, right? I'm wearing a size fourteen! I'm going to interview Prince Harry! This is one of the best days of my life!

Shortly after lunch time, I head to Kensington Palace in my finery with four other *Telegraph* colleagues – two producers, a photographer and a sound recordist. Did all podcasts come with such huge teams behind them, or just the ones featuring members of the royal family? Still, I am grateful for the company. It isn't every day that you find yourself interviewing Prince Harry, and right now their presence seems to be the only thing stopping me from turning into an enormous pile of jelly. We saunter up to the gates in as nonchalant a manner as possible, where two armed policemen half scare us out of our socks by casually turning to us, guns as pointed as their smiles. 'How can we help you today, folks?' one asks.

'We are, err, we're . . .' I try to steel myself and breathe deeply. 'We're here to interview Prince Harry,' I eventually manage to squeak.

And suddenly I feel very, very woozy.

Though that could just be the dress.

*

Something kicks in – adrenaline, self-preservation – and I manage not to faint. As long as my bowels don't pull their usual marathon-training trick, I should be OK.

We are escorted from security through to the palace proper, where we are taken into a smart living room decorated with old paintings. There are two huge sofas that I would totally love in my own house were it not for the presence of a four-year-old who likes to draw on finely upholstered items of furniture. An enormous coffee table sits in between the sofas, covered in coffee-table books. It's then that I twig that this is probably not Prince Harry's actual living room – nobody who actually lives in a living room has a coffee table full of coffee-table books, in my experience; usually they are covered in half-drunk cups of tea and old takeaway leaflets. Or is that just me? The framed and signed pictures of the Duke and Duchess of Cambridge and Prince Harry are another hint that this is their 'public' living room, and for a moment I allow myself to drift off into a daydream in which I too live in a house so big that we can have more than one sitting room – one for receiving guests in, featuring signed pictures of myself, Harry and Edie, and one in which we can slob out watching Netflix. 'Who lives in a house like this?' I imagine Loyd Grossman saying as he goes *Through the Keyhole* of our sumptuous abode. But before he can get to the master bedroom with en suite, I am rudely awoken from my daydream by the photographer.

Eat, Drink, Run.

'Erm, Earth to Bryony?' he says. 'I don't mean to interrupt you but I thought I would just point out a tiny thing before we get going.'

'Yes,' I say, snapping to attention.

'That's a lovely dress you are wearing.'

'Why, thank you so muc—'

'But I can see your black bra through it. Do you want me to try and photoshop that out in the pictures?'

Before I have a chance to answer, Prince Harry has walked into the room.

His Royal Highness is wearing jeans and a grey, cashmere jumper. He looks a little startled when he sees the amount of people in the room, but composes himself as he heads over for a hug. A hug! With Prince Harry! As I stand there with my bra showing through my dress, I try and channel Kimberley instead of Jareth. Kimberley would know what to do in this situation. Kimberley would just swish her sex hair and ride it out. So everyone can see what underwear I am wearing under my dress? SO WHAT? Maybe that was exactly the look I was going for when I got dressed this morning.

I am so thankful to have Kimberley in my armoury: finally an imaginary friend to see off my imaginary foe.

We exchange pleasantries. My colleagues smile like goons. God, people are *so* embarrassing when they first meet royalty. Discreetly, Prince Harry asks if he could speak to me and Jason, his communications director, alone. Jason ushers everyone out of the room. I am beginning to feel a little alarmed. Has he seen my black bra and decided to pull out at the last moment? Oh God, why can't I seem to get *anything* right? But Kimberley tells me to breathe, to listen to what His Royal Highness has to say in a calm manner.

'So I don't mean to sound tricky,' he smiles, 'but I was wondering if it could just be us in the room while I do the interview? It's just I'm a bit nervous about what I am going to say, and the less people there are the easier it will be.' He laughs in a slightly anxious manner.

'Of course!' I say, relief sweeping over me. I pat his arm in what I hope is a reassuring manner. He suddenly looks a lot cheerier. And then it occurs to me: I am calming Prince Harry down. Me. Calming down *Prince Harry*.

What on earth is he about to say?

What follows is an edited transcript of our interview, with the umms and errs edited out to make it as smooth a reading experience as possible.

BG: I'm very excited for our first guest on this podcast, we have Prince Harry.
HRH: Hello.
BG: Hello.

HRH: I'm the first guest, I thought I was, oh okay.

BG: Yeah, you're the first guest.

HRH: Okay.

BG: It's pretty, we've set the bar high.

HRH: Fantastic.

BG: Unless you can ask your Granny if she fancies coming on next week?

HRH: Umm, I think she only signs herself up for video auditions and stuff like that, she's not so into the podcast yet.

BG: Oh well.

HRH: I've got to admit, I don't really listen to podcasts so this could be interesting.

BG: Really?

HRH: Yeah.

BG: Well, it's just like a chat, it's like you know, we're down the pub or something – but we're not, we're in a nice room in Kensington Palace.

HRH: For all the listeners out there just picture that – the old-school paintings on the wall.

BG: There are some signed pictures of you.

HRH: Yeah, there are some signed pictures. No, don't talk about that, that's embarrassing! There's a pot of tea next to me, that's great. [It turns out that this is the room in which the young royals do all their interviews, including the one that Prince Harry does a few months later with Meghan

Markle, to announce their engagement. On the very same sofa!]

BG: Thank you for coming on, it means a lot. What we start the podcast with is by asking people how are you? Really, how are you really right now? Because we ask that question to each other about a hundred times a day, don't we? And we all go, 'Fine, yeah, fine,' but I think that Heads Together and the work you're doing is all about changing the conversation about mental health so can I call you Harry? Can I call you Hazza?

HRH: Call me whatever you want, yep that's fine.

BG: So Hazza . . . How are you today, really?

HRH: Umm. You know what, I have spent most of my life saying 'I'm fine', and I've used exactly the conversation we've just had there as an example with so many other people. People say, 'How are you? How are you?' 'I'm fine, I'm fine . . .' It was a case of just saying fine is so much better than having to go into the details because as soon as you say, 'Oh you know, so and so . . .' then there is another question that follows that and then another question and another question and most of us are not up for going that deep. So today I'm OK. I'm a little bit nervous, a little bit tight in the chest but otherwise fine, ha!

BG: Don't be nervous.

HRH: No, it's understandable.

BG: I won't bite, I promise. So let's talk about Heads Together and the work you are doing. I'm doing the marathon for Heads Together.

HRH: Congratulations about that, by the way.

BG: Which is literally mental. It's the most mental thing I've ever done and I've done some quite mad things.

HRH: [laughs] That's what I've heard.

BG: You guys could have put your name to any charitable cause but why did mental health stand out for you?

HRH: A combination of reasons really. One was the fact that because of all the charity work that William, Catherine and I have been doing, whether that's homelessness, whether it's kids and early intervention and stuff like that, and obviously my connection with the veterans – everywhere we go there is a conversation that happens with someone that we've spoken to that links it into a mental health conversation of sorts. And all of us came and put our heads together – funnily enough – and we thought it would be really good if we could somehow capture the interest of the whole of the UK and make sure we can somehow change the conversation and change the tide on mental health specifically, because it's linked into so many different things. And while all of this was happening we kept meeting people that were struggling. And we thought, well look, the three of us have never come together on an issue, because the idea of working together was probably a little bit daunting but you know what, it's great fun and you know we all have different passions to the cause and we all have different reasons for doing it, and yes, fine, we have personal reasons but the main reason was it seemed to be the right time. People seem to be talking about it. It was written about in newspapers more and more and we just thought, 'Wouldn't it be cool to change the conversation and to get the whole of this country on board?' Because the experience I have had is that once you start talking about it you suddenly realise you're actually part of quite a big club.

BG: Yeah, it's a real community.

HRH: It's a real community and everyone's gagging to talk about it. I don't know whether it is being British and having this stiff upper lip or whether it's just us not being in touch with our emotions or not being cool to talk about it or being a weakness, all this sort of stuff. After whatever it is you know specifically during the last five or six years, after talking with the lads that have left the military and experienced post-traumatic stress, depression, anxiety, panic attacks and

alcoholism, all of that stuff. Having those conversations with those guys it became blindingly
obvious to me that even if it was a small problem
in your youth, something – Afghanistan, in a lot
of these cases – was the trigger for all of these
issues to come forward. It just became obvious to
us that no matter who you are, a conversation has
to happen, that has to be the beginning. Because
otherwise how are you ever going to know who
to see, where to go and how to solve it?

BG: No one has ever got better from a mental
health issue by not talking about it.

HRH: Exactly, and if you stay silent it's more
likely to kill you.

BG: Yeah, you don't have to suffer in silence.

HRH: No, you don't.

BG: And that's the one of four in us, every year,
and that means four in four of us know someone
who is going through something right now. So
you mentioned there were personal reasons. I obviously don't want to be too nosey because I don't
really know you that well.

HRH: Yes you do! [laughs]

BG: Yes I do, obviously I have so many questions.
We have just mentioned the one in four. It is really,
really normal to feel weird. In fact, it is probably
weirder to always feel normal.

HRH: Yes, good point.

BG: I mean, do you have any experience with mental health issues?

HRH: Yeah. I mean I think I have especially over the sort of the beginning of this campaign and, previously, I think if anybody looked at my life, I can't speak for the other two obviously, they have got their own reasons. But for me specifically, if you look back to the fact that I lost my mum at the age of twelve, on a public platform, which it was, and then there's everything else that happens with being in the spotlight and this sort of role and the pressures that come with it, and then going to Afghanistan and then working in the personnel recovery unit with other soldiers as well and taking on a lot of their issues . . . Anyone would look at that and go, 'OK, there must be something wrong with you, you can't be totally normal, there must be something wrong.' And I sort of buried my head in the sand for many, many years.

Some people have written about it and suggested there might be something wrong with me, that it might be Afghanistan-related. I can safely say it's not Afghanistan-related – I'm not one of those guys that has had to see my best mate blown up next to me and have had to apply a tourniquet to both their legs. Luckily, thank God, I wasn't one of those people. But I can safely say that losing my mum at the age of twelve and therefore

233

shutting down all of my emotions for the last twenty years has had a quite serious effect on not only my personal life but my work as well. And it was only three years ago [that it came up], funnily enough from the support around, and my brother saying, 'Look, you really need to deal with this. It is not normal to think that nothing has affected you.'

BG: Is that your way of dealing with it?

HRH: My way of dealing with it was, yeah . . . sticking my head in the sand and refusing to ever think about my mum because why would that help? It's only going to make you sad, it's not going to bring her back. So from an emotional side I was like: right, don't ever let your emotions be part of anything. So I was a typical twenty, twenty-five, twenty-eight-year-old running around going, 'Life is great, life is fine,' and then I started to have a few conversations and actually all of a sudden all of this grief that I had never processed started to come to the forefront. And I was like, there is actually a lot of stuff here that I need to deal with. And that combined with being stuck in certain situations . . . that fight or flight [feeling]. Being in situations when you're at an engagement and not being able to do the flight bit, your body ends up kicking into the fight and yeah . . . I have had some . . .

It was only two years so I can count myself lucky but it was twenty years of not thinking about it and then two years of total chaos. I just couldn't put my finger on it, I didn't know what was wrong with me. I thought it was part of growing up or whatever, and people were just like, 'No, it makes complete sense.' And then once you start talking about it to your mates, two months later those mates were coming back to me, starting a conversation, and in that conversation they would slowly start to unravel their *own* issues because they knew they could; they knew that I could relate to it. And there is nothing better than being able to share your experiences and ask for advice from someone who's actually been through it. Rather than a complete stranger or someone that doesn't get what you have been through.

BG: So do you find doing the Heads Together thing . . . I mean I find when talking about mental health it's not entirely altruistic. There's also an element of hearing other people tell their stories that makes me realise that it's completely normal to feel this way.

HRH: Yeah, totally normal. And I think as I touched on earlier, with the personnel recovery unit with the army, I was going there as a volunteer to go in there and show my support and hear all the stories from these individuals. You know,

235

there was one day when I went there in the morning and sat down with three individuals. One girl who had tried to commit suicide and told me why and how. Another guy who was suffering so badly from post-traumatic stress disorder that he was shaking and blinking and unable to actually make conversation with me. And another guy who had tinnitus from a practice grenade being thrown into a tunnel when he was on exercise in Canada and that tinnitus means that he can't . . . he has to go to bed with his missus with the speaker on playing rain and thunderstorms on every single night because otherwise it's just ringing in his ears all night. And then in the afternoon I was at a WellChild event, meeting terminally sick children and speaking to their parents. And I'm like, 'Aargh . . .'

BG: Yeah.

HRH: So you just park your own issues because of what you are confronted with, and all you want to do is help and listen, but then you walk away going, 'Hang on a second, how the hell am I supposed to process this? I've literally just taken on everybody else's . . .'

BG: You have got to deal with your own stuff.

HRH: You do I think. I have spoken to a couple of psychologists and I say, 'You guys, what is the rule?' I think the rule is like three hours of listening to people is every half an hour of them having to process it themselves to somebody else, because we are not cut out to take on everybody else's emotion unless you are one of those emotionless people who doesn't care. But I got to a point at the age of twenty-eight when I really started to care, I was really uneasy, I was trying to find a path in life and by the age of thirty I was like, wow, this is much better way of life.

BG: Yeah.

HRH: Dealing with all the grief, being able to have that conversation, sharing other people's grief and knowing what they are going through. It's like ok, now I can actually have those conversations with people, and hopefully they can understand that I've got a little bit of experience to be able to share with them and therefore you can have that banter with them, you can make it light hearted when necessary, but also you can be that person there, holding their hand and being a comfort for them when they cry, it's a fascinating process for me that I've been through, not just personally, but all of the people that I get to meet. I'm so fortunate to get to meet these people who have literally turned their lives around and it's all part of a conversation of being able to talk to a brother, a sister, a parent, a colleague or a complete stranger. As I'm sure you know, some of the best, or the easiest people to speak to is a shrink or whoever. I don't know why Americans call them shrinks. Someone you've never met before, you sit down on the sofa and say, listen I don't actually need your advice, can you just listen.

BG: Just listen to me.

HRH: And you just let it all rip.

HRH: I've done that a couple of times.

BG: Why am I not surprised?

HRH: More than a couple of times actually but it was great and I can't believe I've never done it.

BG: I think everyone should do it. I think everyone should be made to do it on the NHS just for their wellbeing.

HRH: Wouldn't it be great? Everyone has a stressful Monday to Friday so wouldn't it be great if everyone has someone to speak to where you can offload all of your week's grief, all of the day to day stuff. Are we allowed to swear on this or not?

BG: Yeah, you can swear.

HRH: Ok. All of the day to day shit that everyone has to put up with because that's, you know, the honest truth. If you can just dump that on a Friday, how much better would our weekends be? Because I can safely say that once I offload my stuff to somebody else, I feel so much better. Now that's not a selfish thing because if you're doing it with someone who is a professional then it's their responsibility to dump the stuff off of them. They're used to all of this sort of stuff, so I know that there's a huge merit in talking about your issues. The only thing about keeping it quiet is that it's only ever going to make it worse not just for you but also for everybody else around you as well because you become a problem and through a lot of my twenties I was a problem.

BG: Really?

HRH: I didn't know how to deal with it. I probably dealt with it in the same way as you. I don't know.

BG: I drank a lot. When I was ill I didn't even know I was ill. I would just kind of bury it. It was that thing of trying to numb out all of the pain and all of the issues and that just makes it worse. I was drinking a lot. With me personally there were drugs involved. It was just like, 'Quieten this down, quieten this down!'

HRH: Yeah, sure.

BG: And then it works in the moment, but a day later it's ten times worse. It's like playing whack-a-mole with your problems.

HRH: Yeah, I know exactly what you mean, it's true. But then even when a loved one or someone really close to you comes up to you and says, 'Look, I think you need to deal with this,' it's all about timing. And for me personally my brother, you know, bless him, he was a huge support to me. He kept saying, 'This is not right, this is not normal. You need to talk about stuff, it's OK.' But the timing wasn't right.

BG: You need to feel it in yourself, right?

HRH: You need to feel it in yourself, you need to find the right person to talk to as well and that's been one of my biggest frustrations and understandings over the last few years – how hard it is to find the right person, the right remedy, because there's so much stuff out there. You have got to find the right person because some people might turn around and laugh. Some people will turn around and go 'Oh, it's not that, it's that.' And, well, that's not helpful because I've spent the last year and a half getting to the point in which I've got to now and you're putting me back sort of a whole year. So yeah, it is timing, it's finding the right person. But I can't – both of us I'm sure – can't encourage people enough to just have the conversation. Because you will be surprised firstly how much support you get and secondly how many people literally are longing for you to come out. You've got so much more in common with some people than you originally thought.

BG: Do you know how much . . . how amazing

it is what you have just said? And honestly I'm not just blowing smoke up your arse.

I remember when I came to the launch of Heads Together last May. I remember I wasn't feeling very well at the time and I remember seeing the kids from Place 2 Be. And they knew everything about depression and I thought, 'God, here are three of the most high-profile people in the whole world talking about mental health,' and I just want to say that was amazing. Because if when I was twelve a similar thing had happened, I wonder how different my life might have been. I really just want to thank you for that because picking mental health . . .

HRH: You know what? No one needs to thank us for that because it is a topic of conversation that was bound to happen anyway. We happened to have nothing on at the time [laughs] and as I say the three of us decided to come together because it is something that we really believe in. And one of the best things – what my mother believed in – is the fact that if you are in a position of privilege and responsibility and if you can put your name to something that you genuinely believe in and other people believe in and if you get that support and that belief and that encouragement, then you can smash any stigma you want and you can encourage anybody to do anything. And I think and I hope that's what Heads Together is proving. This is not about us; this is about every single person out there who is suffering from daily stress, post-traumatic stress, anxiety, alcoholism, depression, whatever it may be. This is why we are doing it. We are doing it for them. We're not doing it for ourselves. But you know, one of the most frustrating things would be to do a campaign like this and not have support of the media and not have support from the public. So I think the stars aligned at the right time and I think it makes complete sense for the three of us to put as much effort and as much passion into this based on a lot of knowledge and experience that we have had, whether it be personal or whether it be official.

BG: What you are doing is taking negatives and turning them into positives and that is awesome.

HRH: Yeah, hopefully with a little bit of humour to it as well. Because I spent ten years in the army and if you sit down and talk to these guys about the issues that they have had, it's all dark humour. Now I know the general public might not agree with that to a certain extent but I can safely say in Headley Court, when these guys go through their rehab, the idea of someone being stuck in bed and being late for breakfast because someone's nicked both of their prosthetic legs is part of the . . . I know, you're laughing!

BG: It's how you get through it.

HRH: It's how you get through it. I'm not suggesting it's how the rest of the general public do that because it probably won't work and I will get crucified for it, but in that specific experience that I've had, it works for these guys. And something else will work for someone else. But what we are trying to do is normalise the conversation to the point where anyone can sit down and have a coffee and just go, 'You know what? I've had a really shit day, can I just tell you about it?' Because then you walk away and it's done. Rather than a week later . . .

BG: It's building up.

HRH: Or twenty years later, when what could have been something small has grown into this beast of a snowball which you can't dislodge, or you can dislodge but it's going to cost you a shed load of money, a lot of time, a lot of heart ache and probably a lot of grief for you, your family and your friends.

BG: So you feel in a good place now?

HRH: I feel . . . Yeah, I do feel in a good place. It's weird because fine yes, I'm a prince, I have a house over my head and the security that I need. I have a car, I have a job that I absolutely love. Previous to that I had a second job that I absolutely loved as well that obviously came to an end for numerous reasons – but I now . . . because of the process I have been through over the past two and a half years, I've now been able to take my work seriously, been able to take my private life seriously as well and be able to put blood, sweat and tears into the things that really make a difference and the things that I think will make a difference to everybody else. You know for me the Invictus Games would have never got off the ground if I had never dealt with all that stuff beforehand.

For me, the privilege comes with a huge amount of responsibility. If you can combine the two and try to make a difference and just be as genuine as possible and hope that everybody else sees that, then you get the support, you get the tidal wave and then you can make a difference. Because you know what would really suck? Being in a position where you should be able to make a difference but people aren't listening to you. I mean, when it gets to that point, probably when George and Charlotte are grown up and if I have children then they become more interesting . . .

BG: Are you kind of looking forward to that though?

HRH: I am looking forward to that, but I think at that point you have to take a back seat. But as long as we are this age and we're still interesting, we want to make as much of a difference as we can for the better and if this Heads Together thing . . . *when* this Heads Together thing is a huge success.

BG: It is a huge success already.

HRH: . . . But then you know what, congratulations to the UK, congratulations to the whole of the UK from Land's End to John o' Groats. Every single person, whether you've been suffering or haven't been suffering. That is a round of applause to us in today's day and age where all sorts of things are happening. I think we should all give ourselves a huge pat on the back for getting Heads Together to this point, for getting the conversation to this point. Forget that it's Heads Together – it's the fact that the campaign will hopefully remove the stigma and therefore pave the way for people to talk about issues. And off the back of that, who knows what happens?

BG: It's so exciting, isn't it?

HRH: It is exciting. Mental health is related to so many different things. It's day-to-day stresses, it's homelessness, it's doing the work with all the HIV.

BG: Yeah.

HRH: And stuff like that, it's all connected. Everybody struggles. We are not robots; we are humans.

Eat, Drink, Run.

BG: It's a no-brainer to invest in mental health on every level. Because it pays off. A happy country is a healthy country and vice versa.

HRH: But imagine if everybody has been sort of wandering around at 50 per cent mental capacity. Imagine what we as a country – I'm going to be cheesy now –

BG: Be cheesy!

HRH: Imagine what we as a country, what we as individuals could achieve by unlocking that next 25 per cent. So we can say, 'You know what, I've cleared my head of all that rubbish that I don't need. So now I can function at 25 per cent more in my job, at home, as a parent, whatever it be.' And that, that is the most unifying thing with everybody as far as I'm concerned. Because it doesn't matter if you are a prince, a mother, a CEO of a company or a white van driver or a kid. It doesn't matter who you are. Mental health, mental *fitness* relates to every single one of us and there's only positives that come out of our talking about it.

BG: So next, do you think you will have children now you are in that good place?

HRH: Yeah, I'm a godfather to quite a few of my friends' kids.

BG: How many are you?

HRH: Err, actually five or six.

BG: Are you a really awesome godfather?

HRH: I'd like to think so. The key to that is to grow up but also be in touch with your . . .

BG: Your childish side.

HRH: Yeah, your childish side. If that means going to someone's house and sitting down and playing PlayStation and kicking the ass of their son on Counter-Strike or Halo or whatever it is then I will try and do that – though I'm actually so out of practice with that. But of course I would love to have kids.

BG: But just quickly . . .

HRH: You haven't even looked at your sheet [of questions].

BG: Because it's just flown by, Harry. How do you stay sane? What are the little things, the little tricks that you do? Do you exercise? Do you secretly Morris dance? What are the things?

HRH: I don't Morris dance.

BG: Oh, that's sad.

HRH: And I play golf really badly.

BG: Really bad golf?

HRH: Only occasionally. And just general exercise. In answer to your question, I have no idea how I or any of us stay sane. When I say me, I talk about our offices as a whole. There is day to day pressure on all of us, and there's day to day pressure on every single person, I get that, but it was . . . you're asking me the questions and I can genuinely say that I don't know how I stay sane. I don't have any secrets though I have probably been very close to a complete breakdown on numerous occasions when all sorts of grief and lies and misconceptions are coming at you from every angle. But, you know, it comes with the job, it comes with the role and one of the hardest things I suppose is not being able to have that voice or being able to stand up for yourself, you have to just let it wash over you, you have to. I hope that we as a family or we as an institution are able to try and remind people about certain core values and standards and the fact you can put up with a huge amount of grief. You shouldn't have to but you can.

And some people have techniques and you know on a very personal level I go running or do a bit of boxing. During those two years I took up boxing because everyone was saying boxing is good for you and it's a really good way of letting out aggression. And that really saved me because I was on the verge of punching someone, so being able to punch someone who had pads was certainly easier.

But exercise is really the key. I mean you're doing the marathon and so many other people doing the marathon for Heads Together for us is such . . . I was going to say a simple solution with which you will disagree [laughs] but what I mean by that is exercise is a simple solution.

BG: Yeah, it is.

HRH: It doesn't matter who you are, you can take up anything. Instead of giving up, giving up, giving up, how about take up, take up, take up? I know that with Lent people are always encouraged to give up things. I always think why don't you take up something because taking up something – whether it is going for a walk if you have time, or instead of taking the tube going for a walk along the river, that kind of stuff – I personally think that makes a huge difference. And if you're lucky enough and have the opportunity to get out of town and out of cities, go and get in touch with nature because that's what it's there for and if we lose touch with that there is no point in keeping it. If there is no point in keeping it then I certainly don't want to be on this planet because it has so many benefits to it.

And as I said, running the marathon . . . What is it? Twenty-six miles?

BG: It's 26.2 miles. It's the point two that's significant.

HRH: Isn't the point two down the Mall in front of Buckingham Palace?

BG: I . . . will . . . Yeah, I will be crawling by that point.

Eat, Drink, Run.

HRH: No you won't, you are going to nail it and probably in under four hours as well.

BG: I do not think so!

HRH: That's it. Guys, did you hear that? Under four hours for Bryony! So um, yeah. I could not encourage people more to take up something. Take up a new hobby, whether it is boxing, sport, going to the gym. Cycling. I know this country is obsessed with cycling. Everyone deals with daily stress. Everyone has their own stress. We have our own stress. Trying to cope with life in general . . . not only is that going to make it better for you, it's going to make it better for everybody else who cares for you and worries about you. So yeah, I don't know what else to say to that.

BG: Harry, thank you so much.

HRH: No, thank you for the chat.

BG: That's been amazing. I feel like, I just . . . I want to clutch you to my bosom but I keep hugging you and it's not cool.

HRH: It's fine. We can have a hug afterwards.

That really did happen. All of it. Seriously. I really did say the word 'arse' in front of Prince Harry, and tell him I wanted to clutch him to my lacy-black-bra-clad bosom, which he could probably see through my dress. He really did say the word 'shit', and admit to the world that he has been close to a breakdown. This man has bravely broken away from all the traditions of the stiff upper lip that his family – the *royal* family, can we not forget – have always epitomised.

I mean: woah. *WOAH.*

No wonder he was so nervous.

My whole life, I have been terrible at keeping anything to myself – other, of course, than my mental illness, and recently even that I couldn't stop talking about at every turn. The moment something exciting happened, I just had to share that excitement with everyone I knew including the man at the corner shop, lest I burst. Even when something embarrassing happened – and embarrassing things seemed to happen all the time to me – I found it impossible to keep it to myself. When I told someone else, the shame somehow dissipated. It was also pre-emptive, in that I was often getting in there and putting myself down before anybody else had a chance to.

But with the Prince Harry interview, I was sworn to secrecy. For three, excruciating weeks, until the Sunday before the marathon, I was going to have to keep the contents of the podcast to myself. The editor had heard it, obviously, and practically done cartwheels in his office, but after that the recording had been put on a USB stick and locked in a safe. No matter how much I wanted to tell everyone that I had just flashed my bra at Prince Harry, I couldn't. Even my own Harry was oblivious to what had happened in that room, on account of the fact that he worked for a rival newspaper. I spent long hours twiddling my thumbs and pacing up and down rooms. 'Would you JUST. SIT. STILL?' my colleagues implored me. But I couldn't. If I sat still, I would almost certainly start to catastrophise about all the ways I could fuck things up before the interview came out: I could accidentally burn down the building containing the safe; I could get drunk and tell a room full of journalists that Prince Harry had given me the interview of his life, prompting them all to try and spoiler it by digging up dirt. And speaking of dirt: what if, when the interview came out, a million bitter columnists wrote scathing pieces about Prince Harry's interviewer being a coke-addict whore-bag? Or was I making the mistake again of presuming the whole world revolved around me?

Some days, it was almost too much to bear. There was nothing for it.

I was going to have to run.

And that was just as well, because I needed to. I had to do one last long run before I 'tapered' – tapering being the weeks just before the marathon where you are instructed to do nothing but sit and rest so that your body is fully prepared for the mad endeavour it is about to take on. When I had initially looked at my training programme all those months ago, I liked the sound of tapering. I imagined, in so much as I could imagine back then, that it would involve lots of cake and massages from my husband. Grapes peeled for me. Being waited on hand and foot, that kind of thing.

But now I was here, tapering terrified me. Tapering was the full stop on marathon training: once you had tapered, there was nothing more you could do. You just had to sit and hope that whatever you had in your legs was enough to carry you through. And what if my fitness suddenly disappeared? What if I spent my tapering period on the sofa eating doughnuts? I had lost almost three stone since the start of marathon training, but it would be just like me to put it all back on in the run-up to the big day, to blimp out big time so that I couldn't even make it to mile one.

'Would you just relax?' said Harry.

'Would you just fuck off?' I snapped back. The stress was getting to me.

Luckily, Tim was going to join me for the last run. It was going to be twenty miles. Twenty miles. Gulp. Though a marathon was six and a bit miles longer than that, you aren't supposed to run the full distance before the big day, and I told myself that six and a bit miles was *only* 10k. I caught myself then. Just four months ago, 10k had seemed like going to the ends of the earth. Now it felt like a nip to the corner shop.

Eat, Drink, Run.

We set off from my house at 6.30 a.m. It is set to be an unseasonably warm early April day, and Tim wants us to get ahead of the heat. Blearily, I eschew my normal morning routine of a fag: I'm not sure smoking is great preparation for what Tim estimates will be four hours of running. Four hours. I feel exhausted just thinking about it.

Running down to the river, I feel quietly confident. Every forty minutes, Tim feeds me water and a gel. We chat. If you want to get to know someone, then may I suggest running long distances with them? I learn that as well as being married to the gorgeous doctor he has three children. That he was once on the Olympic programme, but then he got injured and it all fell apart. That he experienced depression, that he knew the depths of misery the brain can reach at its darkest, hence his keenness to help me. Running along, I cannot help but feel almost grateful for Jareth the Goblin King, for all the people like Tim that he has inadvertently brought into my life.

Soon, I am amazed to find we are in Richmond Park and at the half marathon point. It amazes me how my parameters have changed so quickly, how already thirteen miles feels like very little. The sun is shining and the park's deer graze lazily around us. At fourteen miles, I stop to use the loo and apply more Vaseline to my body. Then we are off again, and it hits me that I couldn't stop even if I wanted to.

Without realising it, I have passed through the physical pain barrier you have with running and into unchartered waters – a mental territory where all that matters is getting to the end. My feet might hurt. My calves might throb. And my energy bank might feel completely empty. But all I care about is putting one foot in front of the other. One foot in front of the other, I repeat again and again. If I stop, I know it is going to be more painful to start again. So I will just keep going.

Along the river we run, to Hampton Court Palace and Bushey Park. We double back and the kilometres pass in a blur of hazy sunshine: 27k, 28k, 29k, 30k . . . just a little bit further and we have done it. Just another ten minutes or so, and I have run twenty miles.

My phone starts bleeping at 9.45 p.m., when the interview is released. At first friends, then news networks. By the time I get to sleep at 1 a.m., I know I have to be up four hours later to do a day of media: BBC, ITV, SKY, CNN, and so on and so on.

Finally, the interview is out and I feel like I can breathe again. The reaction is incredible – my inbox is bursting like never before and I keep hearing my voice on the news as I chat to Prince Harry. Plus, it being a podcast, nobody has mentioned the bra. All week, the news agenda is dominated by His Royal Highness opening up about his mental health issues. Even Theresa May announcing a general election fails

Eat, Drink, Run.

to dampen the enthusiasm everyone seems to have for talking about stuff that just a couple of years ago seemed unspeakable. And over the next few days, on the back of the publicity surrounding the interview, my marathon fundraising total goes from £19,000 to £25,000 and then, incredibly, £33,000.

Now all I have to do is run the bloody thing.

10

To the Starting Line

The morning of the marathon, my period comes.
Of course it does.

It couldn't just hold off for a few hours, wait until I was all done and turn up at some point around tea time, when I would hopefully be somewhere with my feet up and a cold beer in my hands – that somewhere not being a St John's Ambulance, thank you very much. No, it had to rush in and turn up early, which, as you might have guessed, is very unusual when it comes to my body. But even the idea of running with Aunt Flo can't dampen my spirits. I was not going to be the first woman to do a marathon bleeding – or even the first man, given the state of some of the post-race nipples I had seen on running websites – and I was not going to be the last. Indeed, I had even heard about a woman who had decided to 'free bleed' as she took part in the 2016 event, to prove a point. But I was not going to follow her lead. As much as I admired her stance, I didn't fancy the chafing. And as you know, I had become obsessed with chafing.

I would just have to be imaginative, and hand great clutches of tampons to friends and family who were coming to cheer me on. Then they could pass them to me at strategic points. In the meantime, I set about slathering myself in Vaseline. I covered myself in it from top to toe, avoiding only my face, which I had left bare save for a generous coating of waterproof mascara. Even marathon runners had to look good, I had decided, and so the day before I had turned up at my local salon and asked them to braid my hair. That meant I wouldn't spend the whole race being annoyed with it. No matter that I looked like a budget version of Bo Derek in *10* – when I walked out of that salon I certainly felt the part, so much so that I went straight back in and asked them to paint my nails in Heads Together blue.

If I was going to do this, I was going to do this properly.

I laid out my clothes and looked at my feet. After all this training, they weren't pretty. In fact, they were kind of hideous. Great thick calloused layers of skin had built up around them – I noticed the beginnings of a bunion on one toe. Flecks of nail polish that I hadn't bothered to take off since Ibiza covered some of the toenails. But they had done their job. They had taken me this far. Now they just had to get me a tiny bit further.

'Goodbye, toenails,' I said, as I put on my socks. 'Thank you for all you have done for me. It's been fun.' Then I put on my leggings and my Heads Together vest, upon which my name was printed in great big letters.

'Mummy, why are you talking to your toenails?' asked Edie.

'Because she's mad,' said Harry. 'And because she's finally about to do the marathon.'

'Are you really, Mummy, are you?' After all this time, she finally looked excited.

'Yes,' I said, a happy tear in my eye. 'Yes, I think I actually am!'

Tim arrives just before 7 a.m. laden down with a huge backpack. He is my white knight, my saviour. Harry seems pretty chuffed to see him too – it's probably the bromance that developed in Paris, but I like to think that he is also pleased that someone will be looking after his wife on this momentous day.

'Everything you need for today, you put in here,' Tim says, shoving the cavernous sack towards me. For a moment, I can't quite believe what he is saying. I look at him in disbelief. 'Yes, I'm going to run with this thing on my back so that you don't have to worry about carrying stuff around.' That numinous thing is here again, answering my prayers. I start to cry. 'Wait until you've finished the race before you turn on the waterworks,' smiles Tim.

Into the sack I put my tampons and some sanitary towels, just in case. I put a tub of Vaseline in too, and some paracetamol, not to mention the electrical cables for the portable phone charger, all of which join the loo roll Tim has bought along 'in case we get caught short. The portable loos aren't always, you know, equipped.' I look at the contents of the bag and realise that if you didn't know we were about to run a marathon, you'd think we were a pair of perverts.

A few days earlier, Tim and I had gone to the Virgin Money London Marathon expo out at one of those huge, cavernous conference centres that seems to have no end. It was here that we picked up our race packs and numbers, and it was here that the reality of what I was about to do hit me. I was going to run a marathon. There was no backing out now.

The Prince Harry interview seemed to have turned me into a mini-celebrity, and everywhere I went people stopped to tell me how much they appreciated what he had said. I couldn't quite process what was happening, how I had gone from being the girl who felt so alone to this in such a short space of time. All my life I had thought that I had to be thinner, prettier, more talented. But I hadn't – all I had to do was be myself, and do a bit of training for a marathon. That day, it felt to me like anything was possible. 'Get used to it,' said Tim. 'Because on Sunday, you're going to feel like this times infinity.'

In the middle of the expo there was a stage where expert marathon runners were interviewed. I stood and watched as a man who had done five marathons back to back spoke about how he was going to treat himself at the end of London: he was going to allow himself some fish. Before I knew it, I was being whisked up on stage and presented as 'the girl who interviewed Prince Harry'. The man asked me how I planned to treat myself afterwards. 'Um, a pint of beer and a packet of fags?' was all I could think of to say. Some people laughed, but many more didn't. I hoped it wasn't a sign of things to come.

'I just wanted to let you know that my commitment to today is such that I haven't actually had an alcoholic drink or smoked a cigarette for six whole days.' I am in the cab to the start line with Tim, going back over my embarrassing moment on stage. Tim shakes his head and laughs. 'I'm really proud of you, Bryony. Now if you could just hold off while you're actually running the marathon, that would be great.'

My belly is full of porridge and my heart is full of love. As the cab drops us off in Greenwich, and I see the crowds of people making their way towards their start lines, I feel like a kid on Christmas morning. I can barely contain my excitement. I think I might actually burst. Helicopters fly overhead, increasing the buzz in the air. Thousands of runners bustle down roads towards the start point. All these people, all of different shapes and sizes, all with the same goal: to run 26.2 miles. It doesn't matter that some will do it quickly and some will do it slowly, or that some will do it dressed as rhinos. We all have the same thing in common, the same desire: to prove that anything is possible. To prove that you should never say you can't.

And yet I almost can't fathom it, this huge, incomprehensible thing that a year ago I didn't even know I was going to do. My mind flashes back to the Heads Together launch eleven months ago, to how much I have changed since then – both physically and mentally. I think of the times I couldn't get out of bed, the times when I actually fantasised about being run over and not being able to use my legs – these strong, capable and *muscly* legs that today I feel so grateful for. I think of the Mental Health Mates, some of whom have created a giant banner to wave at me today, and I think of all the people who have written to me and sponsored me over the last few months. I think of all of these things, and I want to weep.

Not yet, I tell myself, not yet.

'Are you OK?' asks Tim, perhaps noticing the glass-iness in my eyes.

'Yeah,' I smile. 'I'm OK. In fact, I think I've never been better.'

The London Marathon is so huge that there are various start lines for people to reflect their different speeds. There is also a special one for 'celebrities', and for reasons known only to the organisers, I have been told that this is where I need to be. This means that for the hour or so we have before the race starts, I get to hang around in a tent with all the stars who are doing the marathon – Chris Evans, the man who plays Ian Beale in *EastEnders*, and a variety of people I would recognise if I had recently watched daytime television or *Made in Chelsea*. It's not that I'm above watching daytime television or *Made in Chelsea* – it's just that what with marathon training, Mental Health Mates, being a mum and my day job, I haven't had a chance. Perhaps that will be my treat when I'm done: a day-long binge of *Loose Women* and reality TV.

Nervously, I find myself parading back and forth from the portable loo. It's not that my bowels are being funny today – it's just that I don't want to set off with so much as a drop of urine in my bladder. Interestingly, I notice there is an ashtray in one of the loos, and wonder if I am hallucinating it, so desperate am I for a fag. I bump into Sian Williams and ask her to pop her head round the toilet so that she can confirm the fact I have finally gone mad. 'Nope, you're right, there is an ashtray in the ladies' loo.'

'Do you think this means I can have a cigarette before we start?'

'NO!' shouts Tim.

He is such a spoilsport.

Twenty minutes before start time, Ben from Heads Together appears. 'You again!' I shout, throwing my arms around him.

'Can you believe we're actually here?' he says.

'Not really. But if I think about it too much I might cry. And to think that I nearly missed your email . . .'

'Well, thank God you didn't. Now look, I need to steal you away for a little bit.'

'But the marathon is about to start,' I say, a look of panic spreading across my face.

'There's someone who wants to see you,' Ben announces firmly, and so it is that, with just fifteen minutes to go before I am due to do the most mental thing of my life, I find myself in a private tent, getting a hug from Prince Harry.

'Well *that* was a little bit bigger than we'd expected it to be,' His Royal Highness says, once he has broken away from my iron grip. If I stop holding on to him, might I open my eyes and find it has all been a dream?

I don't want this to end, I don't want this to end; I never, ever want this day to end. And though there have been many firsts over the last year, the one I am experiencing this morning, is, I realise, the biggest of all. Because for the first time in almost thirty-seven years, I have a body and a mind that I am actually proud of. It may be a body covered in cellulite, a body that wobbles when it moves, a body that is covered in scars from chafing. It may be a mind that is sometimes plagued by intrusive thoughts and feelings of self-loathing, a mind that was once addicted to drugs and throwing up food. But it is a mind that a prince feels he can open up to, and a body that can run great distances. And that is enough. Even if I never achieve anything else in life, I realise that is enough.

With just a few minutes to go before 10 a.m., I find myself running to the start line. It is an extra half a kilometre my body could frankly do without today, but given that it came with a hug from Prince Harry, I can't really complain. In fact, as I race back to Tim and we take our places next to the start line and the huge digital clock, I realise that my capacity for whingeing seems to have gone down as my aerobic capacity has gone up. Things I never thought I would write: aerobic capacity gone up, Prince Harry hugged me, I am on the start line of a marathon.

Standing there, looking up at the beautiful blue sky,

Eat, Drink, Run.

I am aware I have tears in my eyes – but they are happy tears. I cannot believe I am here. I cannot believe I am about to move for 26.2 miles, when it feels like just the other day I couldn't get out of bed at all.

And suddenly, above the din of the helicopters and the excited chatter of nervous runners, I hear the sound of someone counting us down. 10, 9, 8, 7, 6, 5, 4, 3, 2 . . . and I swear it can't come soon enough, this magical moment when I finally start the marathon.

It's difficult to describe how strange it feels at first. It's almost as if you're going for a gentle Sunday jog, such is the volume of people you need to get through before you can really start running. Plus, as I remembered from Paris, even then I need to take it slow. Even if I wanted to suddenly show off my sprinting skills, now would not be the time to do it. Instead, I work at becoming one with my fellow runners. We are all in this together, after all. We jog down residential roads, as pacers pass us – these are people with whom you are supposed to run if you are going for a particular time. Mr Three Hours saunters past. Mrs Three and a Half skips off into the distance. Little Miss Four Hours is gone almost as quickly as she appears, and on it goes, until we find ourselves somewhere between Mr Five Hours and Mr Five Hours Fifteen Minutes.

I am aware that this is not about time, that as long

as I manage to get to the finish line within eight hours I will get a medal. But the idea of being out here for longer than six hours fills me with absolute horror. Mental calculations tell me that any longer than that and it will be nearing Edie's tea time, and I don't much fancy still being on the course when everyone else has gone home, including the spectators. For a moment, I have visions of me flailing along the Embankment, a man in a clear-up lorry slowly driving behind me, waiting to scoop me up with the discarded water bottles and empty packets of gels. I imagine my husband standing at the finish line, doing a very slow hand clap as I approach. Then I pull myself back to the present moment. I need to remain positive – I can't be thinking about can'ts at this early stage. Indeed, I am making good time. In fact, remarkably, it seems that five miles have already flown by. Tim announces he needs a pee – easy for him, he can just go behind a tree. I, meanwhile, am hoping that the industrial-strength sanitary protection I have about my person will hold out for another few miles. I decide to take my pace down, so that I don't get too far away from Tim. After about five minutes, I start to panic. Where is he? Has he forsaken me already? Then suddenly I realise he is in *front* of me. 'You can run really fast, can't you, even with that huge backpack on?'

'It doesn't matter what I can do,' he says. 'Today, all that matters is what you can do.'

Eat, Drink, Run.

'Oh, give over with your deep, meaningful quotes and pass me some Vaseline.'

At six miles, somewhere around the *Cutty Sark*, I see Chloe. She is waving a foam finger in the air. Chloe, accessorising with a foam finger and not a martini glass or designer handbag is without doubt the strangest thing I have seen since the ashtray in the ladies' loo that morning. She is screaming my name and . . . could it be that she is crying? I run towards her. Oh my goodness, she *is* crying. 'Are you OK?' I say, throwing my arms around her.

'I'm just so proud!' she says, taking my face in her hands. 'I'm just so fucking proud. Now run. Run for your fucking life, Gordon!'

And that is the first time I burst into tears.

At eight miles, I notice that I have been overtaken by: a man with a washing machine on his back, an 86-year-old on crutches, and around three or four rhinos. I wager that given the increasing heat – it is nudging up towards sixteen degrees, feeling more like seventeen or eighteen out of the shade – they'll regret being so speedy soon. Or perhaps I'm just trying to make myself feel better. Onwards we go. Towards mile ten, I see a young man sitting on the side with his trainers off, rubbing his feet in agony. I want to offer him some Vaseline, but suspect it might be a case of too little, too late.

At mile eleven, as we approach Tower Bridge, the

crowds really start to thicken out. It's incredible, the amount of people who are standing on the side of the road, cheering everyone on. They shout our names and hold up hands for high fives. It occurs to me that in all my time living in this city, I have never seen Londoners so friendly, so welcoming.

While carrying our sack of delights and running along-side me, Tim has also been texting Harry to find out where he is standing. 'They should be coming up soon,' he says. 'So get smiling.' In the distance, I see Edie on my husband's shoulders. She also seems to be crying, though not for the same reason that Chloe was. Indeed, as we go past, Harry is so distracted by Edie's tantrum, that he appears not to see me. I'm wondering if, like the Paris half, it wouldn't have been better if they had both just stayed in bed. But it doesn't matter. Soon I am seeing people at almost every corner. My dad! My uncle! My friend Becca's boyfriend Adam! It's like being in a particu-larly active version of *This Is Your Life*, and I love it.

Just before Tower Bridge, something happens. I start to feel a little faint. 'I think I need to stop and use the loo,' I tell Tim. We run on for a few hundred metres, until we see the next stack of portable loos. A long queue snakes out of them, the kind of queue that is destined to add many minutes to your marathon time. But my need is so bad that I am just going to have to suck it up. Suddenly, we are standing dead still in the line as people run past us.

Eat, Drink, Run.

It's a horrible feeling, like being a small child in a crowd and watching your parents be carried away from you into the distance. I stand and watch the queue, which doesn't appear to be moving. I take the opportunity to put on yet more Vaseline, and wonder if I shouldn't have invested in stocks in it at the beginning of this mad journey. Perhaps this stop is both a blessing and a curse – yes, it will mean we make it round that much slower, but in doing so it will give us a chance to catch my breath. I inhale deeply, try not to panic. Then I am in a cubicle, relieving myself, and it is bliss, such bliss, the nicest wee I have ever done in my whole entire life, including that time I was pregnant and only just made it to the country pub after a long walk. I change my sanitary protection and then exit the loo to find Tim brandishing some antibacterial gel. 'Is there anything you *don't* have in that bag?' I say, in astonishment. 'Are you actually Mary Poppins or something?'

We cross Tower Bridge and it all feels rather magical. Little do I know, it will not feel like this again for a while. On the other side of the road are the elite runners making their way to the finish line – they are at mile twenty-one already. I notice that one of them is running in flip-flops, and wince on his behalf. But even though they are way ahead of us, I wouldn't swap with them for the world. They all look so pained, so miserable, and one of them is actually throwing up over a barrier. Meanwhile, us slowcoaches are taking it all in our stride. We may only be halfway, but at least we seem to be enjoying it.

And yet once we are over Tower Bridge we are into the wastelands of Wapping, and then on our way to Canary Wharf. The grandeur of central London fades behind us, and with it any sense of excitement. The buildings are uglier, the streets more potholed and trickier to navigate. At around mile fifteen, we enter the Limehouse tunnel, and it is here that I feel things start to go wrong. Inside it is dark, and people seem disorientated. It's like a scene from *28 Days Later*, with runners wobbling around in a zombie-like state. My legs begin to feel tired, and the chafing begins to feel real. I take a great big dollop of Vaseline from a member of the St John's Ambulance who is holding out a pot on the side of the road, and shove it down my leggings. Already, I am at the stage of not caring – and yet I still have eleven miles to go.

At mile sixteen, my right leg starts to seize up. My damn abductors again. I think back to Frenchie the Physio, and the miserable weeks I spent on the sofa. I will not let that all be for nothing. 'TIM!' I scream. 'I need painkillers, NOW!' Standing on the road, I take double the recommended dose. It may not be ideal, it may not even be safe, but at the moment I am a deranged lunatic whose only goal is getting over the finish line. Holding on to a barrier for support, I swing my legs back and forth one by one in an attempt to

Eat, Drink, Run.

open my hips out. Then I hear my name being called. Looking up, I see the Mental Health Mates screeching in delight. It is just the tonic I need to get me through the next few miles.

At this point, it all becomes a bit of a blur. I think I hit the wall – a term I had heard often, but not been able to understand. Now I did. Hitting the wall happens when you feel you have nothing left, when you are running on empty and your brain begins to feel like it is dissolving. 'I can't, I can't,' I keep saying as we approach Canary Wharf. Tim stops me, takes my hand. 'Look at me,' he says. 'Look. At. Me. You can. We only say can, remember? You have done so well. You have come so far. We are almost at mile eighteen—'

'I thought it was mile nineteen!' I momentarily feel devastated.

'Yes, nineteen. Sorry. My mistake. We are almost at mile nineteen, and then it's the home run. Then we are nearly there. Then you get that medal and that beer and those fags. Do you hear me?'

'Yes,' I whimper.

'I said: DO YOU HEAR ME?'

'YES!' I scream, and then in the distance I think I see my husband, and once more I dissolve into tears.

Seeing Harry, Edie and my mum and dad is just what I need. It gives me the kind of boost no isotonic gel could deliver – the unmistakeable boost you get when someone you love wraps their arms around you and tells you how proud they are of you. I look at my phone, see all the messages and tweets I have received. A picture I put on Instagram already has 5,000 likes. My email tells me that the fundraising total is now at an incredible £37,000. I see the people on the side of the road, shouting my name in encouragement, handing me Haribos, and I think, 'This ain't so bad, Gordon. This really ain't so bad. You've been through worse than this. Much worse.'

And so at mile twenty-one I decide to pull myself together, and then I realise I am back at Tower Bridge. That it is nearly over. I am giddy. I squeal past the Tower of London, and down to Blackfriars. It is here that I bump into another runner, who also seems to be jumping for joy. 'This is amazing!' she says. 'I loved your interview with Prince Harry. Can I run with you until the end? I've been all alone until now and you're the first person I felt I could talk to.'

And so it is that me and Lorilynn, who comes from Manchester and is running for Cancer Research, hold hands all the way to Westminster, past the Houses of Parliament and the hospital where Edie was born. We run together down Birdcage Walk, and we run together past Buckingham Palace. We run together as the finish line comes into view, and then, before we know what has happened, we are there, we are there, we have done it, and we are holding each other

Eat, Drink, Run.

and sobbing. I don't think I have cried this much since I was a baby.

In just over five hours and fifty-three minutes, I have done it. I have run the London Marathon.

On the Mall, I feel slightly stunned. An official puts a medal round my neck, and I throw my arms around Tim. 'Now you need to drink this,' he says, pulling a two-litre bottle of Evian out of his rucksack. I feel as if I have run the marathon with a superhero.

We walk to the Heads Together reception, where we are keen to grab a quick bite to eat and say hi to the other runners and staff before we head back to mine for celebratory drinks with friends and family. My legs feel strangely fine, but that could just be the adrenaline. 'Do you know something?' says Tim. 'That was way harder than when I ran it in two and a half hours. Being on your feet for that long is seriously tough.'

'Are you saying that I'm hard as nails?'

'You bet I am,' he smiles. And then we head into the reception just off the Mall.

The marathon has taken me so long that by the time we arrive there, the royals have left. But it doesn't matter. I just want to wolf down some pasta, and thank Ben for sending me that email way back when. As we go to walk up some stairs, Jason from Kensington Palace stops me. 'Bryony,' he says, handing me his iPhone. 'There's someone who wants to speak to you.'

I look at the name on his iPhone. It isn't one I recognise. 'I don't know who that is,' I bleat. 'I don't know if I've mentioned, but I've just run a marathon. Can't whoever that is wait until I've eaten some food and drunk a keg of beer?'

Jason laughs. 'No, it can't. Trust me, Bryony. You really want to take this call.' So I do. And there, in a dehydrated, blissed-out state, I have a fifteen-minute conversation with Prince Harry.

In the cab back home, I feel like I am on cloud nine. I have just run a marathon and been personally congratulated for my achievements by a royal, a royal who just a few weeks ago I managed to persuade to talk openly about their mental health. I need to pinch myself to check I am actually awake, I need to slap myself to be sure I am not dreaming. 'Did all of that just happen?' I ask Tim.

'It totally did. And now you need to try and enjoy it.'

Tim opens the door of the taxi. Already, my legs appear to have seized up. I somehow clamber out and note that Tim is walking as if he hasn't just run a marathon. I shrug. The body really is magic. I go to knock on the door, but before I quite manage this it swings open, all my friends and family behind it. 'CONGRATULATIONS, MARATHON RUNNER!'

they squeal. I hear a champagne cork pop. I see Chloe crying again. Then Edie runs up to me and jumps into my arms. I almost collapse in exhaustion, but the love I am feeling right now is keeping me upright.

'Mummy, why did it take you so long to run the marathon?' she says, bringing me back down to earth with exactly the bump I need. 'I found it very boring. And by the way, you didn't win.' She fixes me with a long, hard stare. Then she smiles, shakes her head, and plants a kiss on me. 'But that's OK. Daddy says we have to tell you we love you anyway.'

I burst into tears again, and realise the biggest lesson I have learnt in all of this: that sometimes – most of the time, actually – the best thing to do is just be yourself. To accept your body, and your mind, and never ever be ashamed of it. To be fearlessly, unapologetically *you*.

Acknowledgements

I would like to thank everyone who sponsored me to run the Virgin Money London Marathon. Thanks to you I had the motivation to run 26.2 miles . . . and together you helped me to raise over £42,000 for Heads Together. Legends, the lot of you!

Thank you to all my Mental Health Mates. You ROCK.

Ellie, Joe and Guy, thank you for putting up with me over the last few years. Jane Bruton, Marianne Jones, Vicky Harper and Chris Evans, I could not have done this without you.

To my agent Nelle Andrew and my editor Sarah Emsley for holding my hand. Georgina Moore, Grace Paul, Vicky Abbott and everyone else at Headline for being the best publisher a mad girl could hope for.

Eat, Drink, Run.

Holly Beck, my rehab rock.

The amazing people behind the scenes at Heads Together deserve special thanks for everything they did last year. Thank you Ben Hurley and Sophia Sullivan for being such an absolute delight to work with.

Jason Knauf, you have become a dear friend, and I am endlessly grateful for your continued support. You are super smart and a credit to everyone who employs you.

Rebecca Priestley, I am so glad we ended up sharing that cigarette all those years ago. I can't wait for even more adventures.

And last – but absolutely not least – I would like to thank the Harrys who have dominated my life in the last year. Prince Harry, thank you for trusting me and letting me play a tiny part in changing the way this country deals with mental health issues.

My Harry, thank you for giving me the courage to show all of me, and not just an edited version of it. Edie and I are lucky to have you: a man who isn't scared of strong women.

Tips and advice from Mind

Get active, feel good

Every year, one in four of us will experience a mental health problem. We provide advice and support to empower anyone experiencing a mental health problem and campaign to improve services, raise awareness and promote understanding. As a charity, we rely on donations to continue our work and we are committed to ensuring that everyone experiencing a mental health problem gets support and respect.

Just like physical health, we all have mental health and as our bodies can become unwell, so can our minds. However, having a mental health problem doesn't have to be a barrier to enjoying sport or physical activity – being active can change your life.

Here are some tips from Mind, the mental health charity, on how physical activity can support your mental health and wellbeing.

Struggling to get going?

Try joining a club or class – it's a great way to meet new people and have fun. Or, you could take a friend or family member along for support.

Eat, Drink, Run.

Short of time?
Try a brisk 10-minute walk twice a day. It could just be to the office or school gates. Small increases in activity are easier to maintain and will give you a sense of success.

Explore the outdoors
Outside activities like cycling or gardening can improve your wellbeing, and give you a sense of grounding or perspective.

Pace yourself
Build up gradually. Too much exercise can make stress worse or cause injury. If it motivates you, set challenging but achievable goals.

Racing thoughts?
Getting active can help your mind to relax. Solo sports like running or swimming can help you get some time to yourself to think things over, away from everyday stresses.

Want to clear your head?
Concentrating on playing a team sport or competitive game (like football or tennis) can help you turn your focus away from your worries and it might not even feel like exercise.

Celebrate your achievements
It's important to celebrate any progress you make, big or small. You might want to give yourself a reward whenever you've done well.

In 2014 Mind launched the Get Set to Go programme, supported by Sport England and the National Lottery. The programme aims to improve the lives of people who have mental health problems through access to sport in their local communities.

For more information on Get Set to Go or to seek confidential support from Mind, call our Infoline on 0300 123 3393 or visit mind.org.uk